Climbing Guides to the English Lake District

Edited by J. Wilkinson

Scafell Group

1974

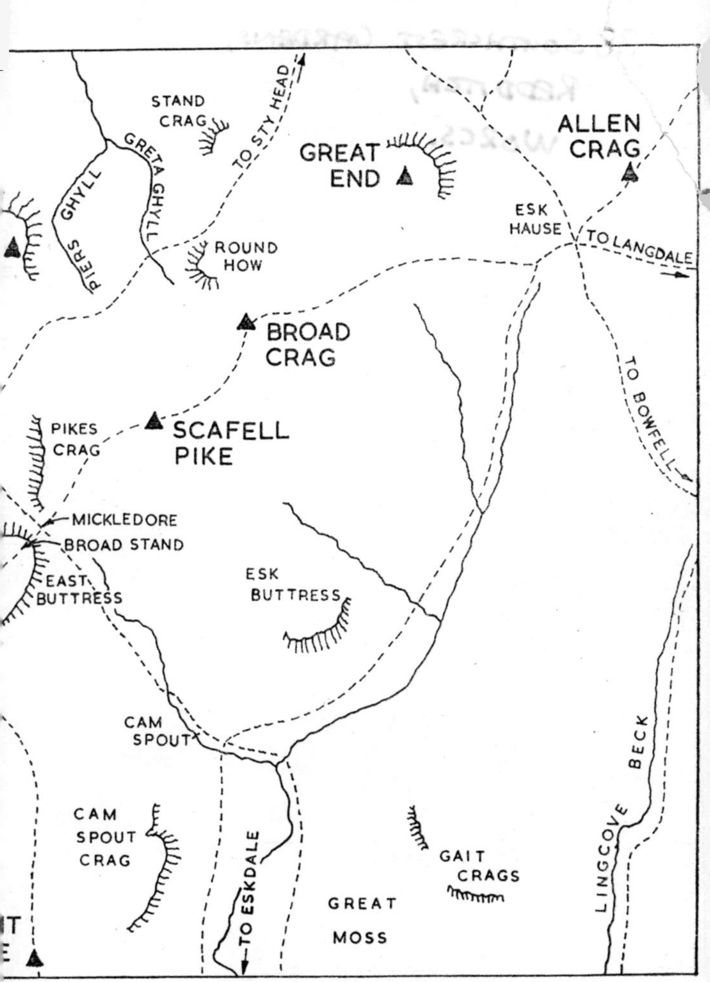

STAND CRAG
TO STY HEAD
GREAT END
ALLEN CRAG
GRETA GHYLL
PIERS GHYLL
ROUND HOW
ESK HAUSE
TO LANGDALE
BROAD CRAG
TO BOWFELL
PIKES CRAG
SCAFELL PIKE
MICKLEDORE
BROAD STAND
EAST BUTTRESS
ESK BUTTRESS
CAM SPOUT
CAM SPOUT CRAG
TO ESKDALE
GAIT CRAGS
GREAT MOSS
LINGCOVE BECK

PETE BARKER,
33 SOUTHCREST GARDENS,
REDDITCH,
WORCS.

The English Lake District

Scafell Group

by M. Burbage and W. Young

Illustrated by
W. Heaton Cooper

Published by the Fell and Rock Climbing Club
of the English Lake District

1SBN 085028 009 5

Scafell Group

Previous Editions of the Scafell Guide:

1924 C. F. Holland

1936 A. T. Hargreaves

1956 A. T. Hargreaves, A. R. Dolphin and R. Miller

1967 G. Oliver and L. J. Griffin

Present edition 1974

Printed by The Cloister Press Ltd., Heaton Mersey, Stockport

Scafell Group

CONTENTS

Scafell Group

EDITOR'S NOTE

That 'Scafell is the Mecca of the climbing world' (an often published phrase), may well be disputed by the devotees of Snowdon and Ben Nevis. Nevertheless, there is no doubt that in the Scafell group there is one of the highest concentrations of magnificent climbs in Britain: certainly nowhere in the Lake District are so many routes of such superlative quality and difficulty to be found. Whilst Langdale and Borrowdale are justifiably popular climbing grounds, mainly due to ease of access and the profusion of low-lying crags, a spell of fine weather is guaranteed to bring the enthusiasts to Scafell.

Since the publication of the last guide in 1967, over forty new climbs have been made in the area, many of them on Scafell itself, and most of them at a very high standard of difficulty. Indeed, over half the climbs in the guide are now in the VS and above categories.

Mike Burbage and Bill Young have done a splendid job on the guide, only a few of the new routes remaining unchecked, mainly on account of the poor conditions on the crags in the late summer of 1973. On behalf of all Lakeland climbers, I should like to thank them for the immense amount of work they have put in.

It is an indication of the scope for further exploration in the Scafell group that splendid new routes are still being climbed without recourse to artificial aids. Long may it be so.

J.W. December, 1973

GENERAL NOTE

Attention is drawn to the following points:

The grading of the climbs in difficulty refers to ascents, and to dry weather conditions and is as follows:

Moderate	Severe
Difficult	Severe (hard)
Difficult (hard)	Very Severe (mild)
Very Difficult	Very Severe
Very Difficult (hard)	Very Severe (hard)
Severe (mild)	Extremely Severe

The pitches have been described in the simplest terms, and any attempt to interfere with the climber's own technique in the art has been avoided as much as possible.

The amount of rope given as required by the leader is net, i.e., the length between him and the second man, leaving out of account waist length. The leader is further advised not to stint himself of rope, especially on the more severe climbs. The length given for each pitch is to the nearest five feet, and is not always the actual height between start and finish, but indicates the length of climbing involved. The same applies to the total lengths of climbs as given.

The angle of a glacis is such that it can be walked up; a slab is steeper; whilst a wall is nearly vertical and may overhang. The slopes are approximately: below 30°, between 30° and 75°, above 75°.

The location of a crag is indicated by its Ordnance Survey grid reference.

The terms 'true left' and 'true right' are used to describe the position of a crag in a valley or ghyll relative to the direction of flow of the stream.

The terms 'left' and 'right', unless otherwise stated, mean as the climber is facing his climb.

Visitors new to the district may find a list of recommended climbs useful.

DIFFICULT/
VERY DIFFICULT
Grooved Arête
High Man via Slingsby's Chimney
Juniper Buttress
Moss Ghyll

SEVERE
Direct from Lord's Rake to Hopkinson's Cairn
Jones's Route Direct from Lord's Rake
Woodhead's Climb

SEVERE (Hard)/
VERY SEVERE (Mild)
Bridge's Route
Great Eastern
Hopkinson's Gully
Morning Wall
Moss Ghyll Grooves
Moss Ledge Direct with continuation to High Man via Herford's Slab and Bad Corner

VERY SEVERE
Botterill's Slab
Great Central Route
Gremlin's Groove
Mickledore Grooves
Slab and Groove
The Fulcrum

VERY SEVERE (Hard)
The Centaur
Central Buttress
Great Eastern (Yellow Slab Variation)
Hell's Groove
The Red Edge
Trespasser Groove

EXTREMELY SEVERE
Central Pillar
Ichabod
Minotaur
Nazgul
Phoenix

Scafell Group

PREFATORY NOTE

We would like to thank all those who have helped us ease the task of preparing this Guide, namely; John Wilkinson, Guide's Editor, who is now in his second series of Guides, a mammoth task, together with; C. Read, J. Adams, G. Oliver, W. A. Barnes, A. Jackman and I. Singleton, all of whom were active on the crags.

Our last acknowledgement is to the previous Scafell Guide authors, C. F. Holland, A. T. Hargreaves, A. R. Dolphin, R. Miller, L. J. Griffin and G. Oliver. It has been a privilege to carry on their work.

M.B., W.Y.

November, 1973

HISTORICAL NOTES

It is probable that the sight of the great cliffs of the Scafell massif has sent a thrill of awe to the hearts of more human beings than any other scene of savage grandeur in the British Isles. For the climber there is still an atmosphere of romance, not only from what has been done in the past, the historic wanderings of the pioneers over these rock faces, but also from the feeling that there are secrets that the mountain has kept through all these years, secrets that it may yet fall to our lot to discover, and that even so there will still be further secrets behind these, so that generations of climbers to come will gaze at these cliffs with the questioning look of those who wish to ascend by hitherto untrodden ways.

And in our contemplation there is an element of wistfulness, as there must be in the contemplation of any great climbing ground, but especially here, in the memories of those who loved these crags and are no longer with us, but whose names will for ever be associated with these cliffs and share their glamour.

Looking backward over the years of exploration, it is noticeable that progress has been made by a series of waves as the technique of rock-climbing has improved, and that no one now believes, as many believed after the great advance of 1911, that the high-water mark has been reached or that exploration has now reached its limit. The history of Scafell proves conclusively that climbing is definitely progressive, not only in the number of its adherents, but also in the standard of achievement which is today higher than that which any earlier generation has reached.

The beginnings are modest; probably the first reference in print will be found in the *Penny Magazine* of 1837, which states the fact that shepherds knew of a way of getting from Mickledore on to the Broad Stand. This was described by

Professor Tyndall in the *Saturday Review* of 1859 as 'a pleasant bit of mountain practice and nothing more.'

The year 1869* marked the first definite advance when no less than three fresh ways of approach were discovered, Major Cundill finding the North Climb; W. P. Haskett-Smith, Petty's Rift; and C. W. Dymond climbing Mickledore Chimney.

Things moved slowly in those days and apparently for thirteen years nothing happened, but in 1882 Deep Ghyll was climbed.

The vintage year of 1869 was marked by an entry in the Visitors' Book at Wasdale Head which reads as follows: 'The attention of mountaineers is called to a rock on Scafell on the right, looking down, of a remarkable ghyll which cleaves the rocks of Scafell. It looks stiff.' And so, thirteen years later, this remarkable ghyll is climbed, first down in heavy snow, the first ascent taking place later on in the same year, while the rock on the right, now known as the Pinnacle, was climbed for the first time in 1884 by Mr. Haskett-Smith without the use of 'ropes or other illegitimate means'. This is now known as the Easy Route, but within a few days a far harder ascent by way of Steep Ghyll, Low Man, and High Man, was accomplished, a remarkable performance whatever route was taken.

In 1888 the ever popular Slingsby's Route was worked out; but 1887 produced one of those *tours de force* which will always be spoken of with bated breath, when C. Hopkinson led a party, under icy conditions, a very considerable distance up the Pinnacle Face, a route now known as Hopkinson's Gully, though the word gully is hardly applicable to it.

During the next few years a series of assaults were made on Moss Ghyll, which fell finally in 1892, and Dr. Collier made, the next year, the amazing little climb named after him, of which the first pitch still defeats advanced experts. In 1896

*There seems to be an error here in associating Haskett-Smith with 1869: born in 1861 he would be only 8 years old in 1869. (Ed. note, 1956).

O. G. Jones made his route up the Pinnacle from Deep Ghyll, and 1897 saw the easterly wing of the crags opened up still further by the Keswick Brothers' Climb.

1898 may fairly claim to be a vintage year through O. G. Jones's magnificent performance in ascending directly from Lord's Rake to the Waiting Room, and so by way of the Mantelshelf to the Crevasse. It would be intensely interesting if one could become clairvoyant and see the route taken by Jones, crawling up thos slabs in his stockinged feet as the evening shadows gathered; the exact line taken can never be known, but the climb was an epic. In the same year Pisgah Buttress was climbed, the West Wall Route found, and Jones and Collier traversed the Pinnacle wall above Deep Ghyll. About this time the first great wave seems to have spent its force and a decade was to elapse before the next arrived.

It is true that 1903 was notable for F. Botterill's amazing lead up what is now known as Botterill's Slab, but in the same year a great set-back was suffered in the accident on the Pinnacle Face during the attempt to reach Hopkinson's Cairn from Lord's Rake, and for some years this spot was avoided by climbers. Jones's route by the Mantelshelf was taken to be a phenomenal effort by a phenomenal climber, and this section of the cliff was set down as unjustifiably dangerous.

But in 1911 S. W. Herford and G. S. Sanson started their assaults on the hitherto impregnable fortress, and by 1914, this and many other citadels had fallen before the prowess of these Shock Troops. On their first objective, the Pinnacle Face, they did not leave much to be done by future explorers as they made the second ascent of Jones's climb; reached the reputedly inaccessible Hopkinson's Cairn from the Rake; entered the Waiting Room by way of Hopkinson's Gully; and worked out most of the variations possible on the expanse of rock between the Gangway and Moss Ledge. They then started the modern fashion of girdling, and after wanderings innumerable the

Girdle Traverse was completed, Though finality seemed to have been attained, the lure of the tremendously vertical cliffs of the Central Buttress proved irresistible and their ascent in the spring before the outbreak of war was a worthy climax to what was up to that time incomparably the most brilliant example of intensive rock-climbing ever seen on British climbing grounds. Its influence on future rock-climbing was profound.

In 1919 a new wave of exploration began. Two new routes to the Waiting Room from Steep Ghyll were found; a direct ascent of Pisgah Buttress was forced; and new routes of high severity were worked out on the walls of Deep Ghyll. Also a magnificent route up the Pinnacle Face direct to Moss Ledge (Fergus Graham). In 1926 one of the finest climbs of all was led by H. M. Kelly and christened Moss Ghyll Grooves. This climb had been projected in 1919, but had defeated the assaulting party, led though it was by the eventual victor.

Faced by the threat of exhaustion on the crags of Scafell facing Wasdale and the sea, the most recent wave realised the potentialities of the long line of cliffs on the far side of Mickledore, with their formidable bulges and overhanging bastions, and a series of new routes, first by Kirkus, then Linnell and A. T. Hargreaves, was started, beside the severity of which the once supreme Pinnacle Face climbs reach a standard of little more than ordinary difficulty, and even the Central Buttress has to bend the knee as far as technical difficulty is concerned, although as an expedition the latter will probably always hold its place as the finest of all the district has in its gift. The Girdle Traverse of this, our newest climbing ground, has yet to be made, and certainly there are other routes here to be added before long, while the wetness and ubiquitously vertical character of this region may well give it the right to challenge the present supremacy of Clogwyn d'ur Arddu, as the wettest, most dangerous, and altogether most formidable crag in the British Isles.

And so we leave the history of Scafell at a time when the future is bright with the possibility of great developments, a time when there is no danger of the call of Ichabod, a time when we may well feel that the best is yet to come.

C. F. Holland, 1936

1933-1967

The early thirties saw the opening of a new phase in the development of Scafell, mainly through the efforts of Maurice Linnell and Colin Kirkus, who were also engaged in comparable activities on Clogwyn d'ur Arddu. Kirkus, a master of delicate slabs pulled aside the veil of mystery from the East Buttress with his ascent of Mickledore Grooves, now a classic, whilst Linnell climbed the now equally popular Great Eastern, a route with wonderful situations yet without extreme difficulty. Linnell went on, with A. T. Hargreaves, to pioneer other routes on the East Buttress. before his unfortunate death in 1934 robbed the climbing world of one of its most gifted performers.

No further advances were made on the East Buttress until the arrival, in 1938, of Jim Birkett, a local man who was to dominate Lakeland climbing for the next ten years. His first sorties resulted in the climbing of May Day, and later the same year he and L. Muscroft girdled the crag, an expedition of over 700 feet of first class climbing.

Little climbing was done during the period 1940–45 but, at the close of the war, Birkett was back on Scafell directing his energies, with great effect, at the Esk Buttress where he recorded no fewer than ten new climbs leaving, apparently, nothing for those who followed. His last route on Scafell, and one of his best, was Slab and Groove, a delicate climb trending leftwards from Moss Ghyll, an area formerly dismissed as worked out.

The Birkett monpoloy of Scafell was broken in 1947 by the Yorkshire school of climbers, led by Arthur Dolphin; Hell's

Groove in 1952 was a standard harder than the existing East Buttress climbs, and in keeping with the advances being made simultaneously by the Rock and Ice Club in North Wales.

Trinity and Phoenix, climbs of a comparable standard to Hell's Groove, were later added by Rock and Ice members and again the sceptics said that all possible lines were accounted for. However, in 1958, they were made to revise their views when a border raid led by the Edinburgh climber Robin Smith established two new and very good routes close to Mickledore Grooves. This sparked off renewed activity among the 'locals' who, over the next few years, filled in several of the gaps on the East Buttress including (thanks to a drought in 1959) two of the last 'wet' problems of Scafell.

This last burst of exploratory zeal took in even the traditional stamping grounds of the Pinnacle Face where some surprisingly fine routes were found. In the forefront at this time was Les Brown, who climbed routes on both faces of Scafell, notably The Centaur, a masterpiece of route finding and Armageddon, the name of which speaks for itself. (Geoff Oliver has modestly chosen to ignore his own fine contributions of which Ichabod undoubtedly ranks as one of the great climbs of the district — Editor.)

The Esk Buttress did not escape the notice of the 'moderns', the extremely bold leads of the Red Edge, and Central Pillar by Alan Austin and Pete Crewe respectively, being the major routes. The latest crag to attract attention has been Cam Spout Crag where there are now several routes which provide good climbing when the higher crags are out of condition.

There are still new lines to explore on Scafell, protected more by their isolated situation than their difficulty, so should the Mickledore chairlift ever become a reality, let Scafell beware !

G. Oliver, 1967

1967-1973

During the six years since the guide was last published, there has been quite a lot of activity in the area, with over forty new routes climbed. However, few are of great importance compared with those of earlier years, but most are quite independent lines, a factor which seems to be lacking in new routes in the valleys, as rock to climb runs out.

1967 was a very poor year, mainly due to bad weather. A companion route to Red Edge on Esk Buttress, Hydra was the only route of note that year. 1968 saw renewed activity, with more new routes put up than in any year since the guide was first published. Three of these routes, all on the East Buttress were all noteworthy additions; Dyad, The Fulcrum and Minotaur. The last two were excellent free climbs on sound rock. 1969 was almost as good a year as 1968. Five new routes were put up on Cam Spout Crag, to more than double the number of climbs on this infrequently-visited crag. On the East Buttress, Read and Adams solved a long-standing last great problem, with a left to right girdle, Lord of the Rings, which crosses some of the most impressive rock in the Lake District. Read together with Lake also added another worthy route on Shamrock, Gilt Edge Eliminate. On the north face of Scafell, two routes of note were added, by Chris Bonnington in 1971 : White Wizard and Central Buttress Girdle. Elsewhere on the north face, several interesting routes were made on the walls of the gullies.

The last two years have been similar in that very few new routes have been climbed. Is it the start of a permanent decline in the Scafell Group or just another lull? One thing is certain however, classic routes which use little or no aid are becoming more of a rarity each year. Will this trend be reversed by a new and more skilfull breed of climbers, in the future? Will they be able to overcome the apparently unclimbable expanses of rock that still remain, without having to resort to artificial aids? Time alone will tell. M. Burbage, November 1973

SCAFELL

The Approaches

The crags of Scafell and Pike's Crag, rock-walls of the mountains forming the hub of the grandest section of the Lake District, are accessible from the valleys of Eskdale, Wasdale, and Borrowdale, all of which radiate from the massif. Langdale, though somewhat distant, may also be considered a centre. The 1-inch Ordnance Survey Map to the Lake District, or the similar Bartholomew, will be useful.

Wasdale.—From the hotel, the road is followed down towards the lake for about a quarter of a mile. Just after passing the old school, there is a gate on the left, with a signpost 'To Scafell'. The path goes through the gate and over the meadow, and crosses Lingmell Beck by a footbridge. The well-marked track now turns sharply to the right, slanting up the side and round the shoulder of Lingmell, crossing several iron stiles *en route.* Shortly after passing the last of these, the left branch of Lingmell Ghyll is crossed. It now mounts the steep grass ridge (Brown Tongue) between the two streams. At the top of this tiring section the path becomes rather ill-defined, though cairned. Here it should be noted that the more prominently cairned route, which ultimately swings away to the left, is the tourist path to Scafell Pike, and extra care should be taken to avoid it in misty weather. The correct route turns slightly to the right towards the crags and crosses a smooth turfy section, leaving a well-marked hollow, filled with boulders of all sizes, on the left. The whole of this area is known as Hollow Stones. The compact mass of dark rock in full view away on the right is Black Crag, the route to which is obvious. The approach to Scafell is slightly left up a green ridge on the right of a well-marked watercourse (often dried up in summer), to a large boulder at the top of Hollow Stones. The crags are now in full view, Pike's Crag being straight ahead up the gently sloping floor of the combe, whilst, linked to it by the sharp-cut gap of Mickledore, Scafell towers grandly on the right. From the boulder, probably the easiest way to Scafell Crag is to continue a short distance, then turn up to the right under the fan of scree coming down from Lord's Rake, and mount, by grass and more stable scree, its left side, working gradually to the right. Rake's Progress is reached near the cross cut in the rock by the entrance to Lord's Rake. Time, one and a half to two hours from Wasdale.

For Mickledore Ridge and the East Buttress of Scafell, continue from the large boulder across the floor of the combe in the direction of Mickledore Screes, bearing up to the right. The last steep and loose section may be avoided by walking underneath the Scafell crags, where a path will be found.

Borrowdale.—The walk to Scafell from this valley is particularly fine. The ordinary tourist route is followed to the top of Styhead, from which the objective is the col between Scafell Pike and Lingmell. The cairned path, which has been named the Corridor Route, keeps well up the slopes of Great End and Broad Crag, and goes along a natural shelf above the deep-cut sections of Greta and Pier's Ghylls. At the col the Wasdale track to Scafell Pike is crossed. The Scafell path continues almost horizontally, passing just below Pike's Crag, to the grass floor of the combe below Mickledore. Time, two to two and a half hours from Seathwaite.

Langdale.—This is the most distant centre. The best way is up Rossett Ghyll to Esk Hause and over the top of Scafell Pike. The path is very well marked and cairned every few yards. From the cairn on the top of the Pike another path drops down in a south-westerly direction to Mickledore. To reach any of the Scafell climbs, follow Mickledore Ridge until it abuts against the rocks of Scafell. This point is the left-hand end of Rake's Progress. For Pike's Crag a descent of about two hundred feet of any of the scree shoots running from

Mickledore to the north-east, brings the crag into view on the right. Time about three hours.

Another route from Langdale, which can only be recommended to strong walkers, is to take the Bowfell Band, pass over the gap by Three Tarns, and, keeping well up, cross the ridge that runs down from Esk Pike. A considerable descent is then made to Cam Spout and the path which starts on the right of the waterfall is followed to Mickledore.

If transport is available, drive to Cockley Beck from where an easy, though often wet, walk up Mosedale leads to Lingcove Beck. Contour below Long Crag and Gait Crags then make for Cam Spout and join the track to the right of the waterfall. Two hours to Mickledore from Cockley Beck.

Eskdale.—From the Woolpack Inn, the best and easiest way to Mickledore is to follow the main road up Eskdale, turning at Wha House up a grass-grown cart road to Taw House. Passing through a gate on the left, a well-marked track runs behind the wall. It crosses Cowcove Beck by a bridge, and soon after turns up the slope to the left. Then follows a gently rising moorland walk for about two miles to near Cam Spout. Probably the best way to Mickledore is to pass close by the toe of Cam Spout crag when a fairly well-marked path can again be taken and followed up the steeply rising hollow to Mickledore. Time, two and a half to three hours.

Alternative route to Cam Spout. After crossing Cowcove Beck, instead of turning up the slope to the left, continue along the path which leads down to the river. At Throstlegarth the river is crossed, and its right bank (true left) is taken overlooking a fine ravine. A magnificent view of Scafell and Esk Buttress is seen through a rock gateway and lightens the walk over a very wet bog to Cam Spout.

It is also possible to reach Lord's Rake via the top of Red Ghyll from Burnmoor. This route is long and tiring and not particularly interesting. The 'White Stones' track starts from the back of the Woolpack Inn. When the track crosses the stream issuing from Burnmoor Tarn, it is time to turn right up the shoulder of Scafell. There is no well-marked track, but by keeping Hardrigg Ghyll well to the left, Lord's Rake may be reached by the top of Red Ghyll. For the top of Deep Ghyll, continue on and pass just under the summit cairn.

Topographical

Scafell Crag is the rampart of rock which forms the north and east faces of the mountain. It is separated from its neighbour, Scafell Pike, by the deep gap of Mickledore. The broad westerly face of the Pike is topped by Pike's Crag. The best view of the crag is obtained from a little above the large boulder at the top of Hollow Stones. Practically the whole mass is seen from here, except, of course, the East Buttress, which is behind Mickledore. It consists of six buttresses. Starting from Mickledore, the first is bounded by the light coloured wall of Botterill's Slab. The magnificent and nearly vertical cliff of Central Buttress is cut off from the next buttress, Pisgah, by the gully of Moss Ghyll. Steep Ghyll is to the right of Pisgah, and the Pinnacle is the fine nose of rock whose right wall forms one side of the broad, well-cut gully of Deep Ghyll. The next wide buttress with low-flung west shoulder is Deep Ghyll Buttress.

Lord's Rake.—From the foot of the Pinnacle, running up to the right, at right angles to, and past the entrance of Deep Ghyll, is a long scree-filled cleft, Lord's Rake. In front of it, and partially masking Deep Ghyll Buttress, is the Scafell Shamrock, its foot reaching down almost to Hollow Stones. Lord's Rake runs up over two small cols, past the starts of several climbs, until it finishes on the Scafell ridge near Red Ghyll. Just below the first col of Lord's Rake, a path turns off to the left over ledges on Deep Ghyll Buttress, and leads into the upper part of Deep Ghyll, above its two pitches. It is a convenient means of reaching the climbs on the walls of Deep Ghyll and a quick way down from climbs in the vicinity. It is known as the West Wall Traverse.

Rake's Progress.—Near the entrance to Lord's Rake, a cross has been carved in the foot of the Pinnacle to commemorate the accident in 1903. It is easily reached from Hollow Stones and is the spot to make for. (See Approaches.) From here, a continuous terrace, known as Rake's Progress runs off to the left. After a sharp little rise, it goes over several shelves of rock past the foot of Pisgah Buttress and Moss Ghyll, and continues just below the steepest part of the crag to Mickledore. From this terrace most of the climbs start. As there is steep rock below the Progress, its passage, especially in one or two places near the Mickledore end, requires care, particularly by novices in wet or windy weather. The cliff below the Progress is too loose to be of any interest except near Moss Ghyll, which has an interesting preliminary pitch finishing on the terrace.

Pinnacle Terrace.—From the entrance to Moss Ghyll and slanting up to the right underneath Pisgah and the Pinnacle, is a series of connected shelves that form another terrace. The Pinnacle Face climbs start from that portion of it which lies between Steep Ghyll and Deep Ghyll.

There is another well-defined and simple path that branches off Rake's Progress to the left, just after its first little rise. It keeps below the steep rocks, on scree, and is altogether less exposed than the Progress. It is the simplest connection between Lord's Rake and Mickledore.

The East Buttress of Scafell is reached by crossing Mickledore and dropping down the scree on the Eskdale side, past Broad Stand and Mickledore Chimney. The buttress overhangs considerably at the foot and looks almost impregnable.

CLIMBS ON SCAFELL WEST OF MICKLEDORE

SCAFELL CRAG

North or Penrith Climb. 30 feet. Moderate. 12 paces to the right from the highest point of Rake's Progress, near Mickledore, is a square recess guarded by a 10 foot wall.

Entry is made on the right and is awkward. Once the shelf is reached the rest is easy. The exit is up the left-hand corner. In descent it is easier to use the chimney below the left end of the recess. This is known as Petty's Rift.

The Hanging Chimney. 120 feet. Very severe (hard).
A short but serious climb starting midway between Petty's Rift and Collier's Climb.
120 feet. From a pile of blocks traverse to the right to a thin break beneath the chimney. Climb up strenuously (one piton in place) to the chimney which is difficult to enter (loose blocks). The exit holds are good however and easier rocks lead to the scree above Broad Stand.

Collier's Climb. 200 feet. Severe (hard), first pitch only, rest difficult.

Starts up a vertical opening in the rocks about 40 yards right of Petty's Rift.

1 30 feet. A vertical scoop is climbed with difficulty until a vertical chimney leads to a large ledge and belay. This pitch is mossy, loose and usually wet. The ledge may also be reached by climbing the first two pitches of Keswick Brothers' Climb.

2 40 feet. The chimney at the left end of the ledge.

3 20 feet. An easy slab running up to the right. Belay.

4 30 feet. Easy ledges lead into a large hollow. Belay on the left.

5 40 feet. The chimney can be climbed direct or entered by an upward traverse from the corner on the left to a stance on a wedged block. Easy exit on the left if desired.

6 40 feet. The chimney leads to the scree above Broad Stand.

Keswick Brothers' Climb. 190 feet. Very difficult.

A somewhat exposed climb. Starts below and to the right of Collier's Climb, where a crevassed ledge leads across the foot of the steep wall.

1 35 feet. Traverse 20 feet along the ledge, step round and ascend 15 ft to a block belay.

2 30 feet. Continue on good holds straight ahead to a ledge and belays.

3 20 feet. Walk along the ledge to the right and climb a short chimney, finishing at the Pulpit.

4 25 feet. Traverse upwards and to the right, across an awkward corner, to a stance and thread belay below an overhanging short crack.

5 15 feet. The crack leads to a large ledge with belays. (Top of Botterill's Slab.)

6 20 feet. Climb up into the gully on the right.

7 45 feet. Easier climbing in the gully leads to scree and boulders above Broad Stand.

Variation Finish.

7a 60 feet. At the level of a large ledge on the right, a 10 foot traverse leads across the left wall to a corner. The corner on the arête is climbed and scrambling leads to the top.

Variation Finish. Severe (mild). Starts from the large ledge on the right.

7b 30 feet. A steep chimney leads to a ledge with belay.

8b 20 feet. The little impending wall above is very difficult.

9b 25 feet. Corners on the right lead to a belay below a slightly overhanging crack.

10b 35 feet. A difficult pull-up is followed by easier slabs.

Tricouni Slab. 60 feet. Severe (mild)

The climb runs up a miniature Botterill's Slab just right of the start of Keswick Brothers' Climb and is in fact, an alternative start to that climb.

1 20 feet. From Rake's Progress, climb a few feet into a recess sheltered by an overhanging wall; then ascend the slab on the left to a stance and belay.

2 40 feet. Continue up the slabs, which get narrower until they merge into the ledge above pitch 2 of Keswick Brothers' climb. Belay.

Botterill's Slab. 140 feet. Very severe.

An attractive climb up the narrow light coloured slab flanking the wall of Central Buttress on its left. 120 feet of rope is necessary to reach a substantial belay above pitch 2. Starts at an opening in the rocks below the foot of the slab.

1 50 feet. Climb a short chimney and continue in the same line for 40 feet. A move to a ledge on the right is then made, and the ledge followed back to the foot of the slab. Good belay high up in the crack on the right of the slab.

2 90 feet. Work out to the left edge of the slab, then back to the face and up for a few feet. Two little corners on the edge lead to a good niche. After a few more feet on the slab, a ledge is reached which leads to the chimney on the right. The direct ascent of the slab is strongly recommended, but since this involves a long delicate pitch, a detour along the ledge to the chimney is advisable to obtain a running belay. An easier alternative is to climb the chimney to a large ledge at the top of the slab, where it joins the Keswick Brothers' Climb. Belay.

Finish up the easy gully on the right, which is the actual continuation of the chimney, (Keswick Brothers' Climb, pitches 6 and 7).

The White Wizard. 330 feet. Extremely severe.
This difficult and exposed climb takes a direct line between Botterill's Slab and Nazgul. Start at the foot of Botterill's Slab.

1 50 feet. Pitch 1 of Botterill's Slab.

2 80 feet. Climb the corner for a few feet until a long stride to the right leads to an impending crack, which is climbed with one nut for aid to a small ledge. Continue up the left-hand crack (1 piton and two nuts for aid) to a good ledge.

3 75 feet. Make an awkward mantelshelf move on to a ledge on the arête to the right; then climb another mantelshelf on to a narrow ledge, which leads rightwards to a crack. Climb this to the gangway, which leads diagonally left to another good ledge.

4 50 feet. Step back down the gangway for a few feet until it is possible to move right, and then up to a very narrow ledge, which is followed by a delicate move back left, to the bottom of a prominent overhanging crack. Climb this to a square-cut ledge.

5 75 feet. Pull up round the arête on right with aid of a piton (still in place), and continue up the groove to the right (nut for aid) to small ledge; then step up, delicately, round the bulge to the right, until easier climbing leads to the top.

Direct Finish. 100 feet. Extremely severe.
Starts at the top of pitch 4 and takes the obvious overhanging corner crack.

5a 30 feet. Climb the corner crack on jams throughout (poor protection). Piton belay on a very large ledge.

6a 70 feet. Go along the ledge to the short corner crack, climb it and continue to the top, (nut belays).

The Nazgul. 260 feet. Extremely severe.
A direct line up the steep wall to the left of Central Buttress. A modern solution to an outstanding problem. Starts at a short crack to the right of Botterill's Slab.

1 50 feet. Climb the crack and ascend easily rightwards by grass ledges to a flake belay below a green crack slanting left. (This crack is actually the left-hand side of the Great Flake of Central Buttress).

2 70 feet. Two pitons are used for aid in the first 20 feet. Step left from the belay to the foot of the crack. With aid from a sling on the first piton (in place) make a difficult finger-pull to insert a nut runner in the crack above. Use this to gain the second piton (in place). Climb the still overhanging wall on reasonable holds to a resting place below a niche. Climb into the niche, avoiding a loose block, and as soon as possible, swing on to a narrow slab on the left. Climb this until easier ground leads to a large pedestal. Belay.

3 15 feet. From the top of the pedestal climb directly up to a flake belay on Central Buttress.

4 25 feet. Descend a little and make a delicate traverse to the right to a right-angled corner, which is climbed to the V-ledge. Belay up on the left. (Part of pitch 6, Central Buttress).

5 40 feet. From the belay go left to a thin crack. Climb this for 25 feet to a good stance. Piton belay. (The first few

feet of this pitch are shared with the Direct Finish to Central Buttress).

6 60 feet. Step left on to the lower of two slabs and climb it to a bulge, which is surmounted to reach the upper slab. The narrowing slab, which is climbed with increasing difficulty, leads to easy scrambling.

Central Buttress. 475 feet. Very severe (hard).

Probably the most famous climb in Lakeland, it combines tradition with difficulty, and though no longer the most serious route on the mountain, it is certainly the most popular. Combined with the Direct Start and the Direct Finish (which leave the best pitches intact), a magnificent climb of unrelenting difficulty may be enjoyed. Starts from Rake's Progress about 50 feet left of Moss Ghyll, up the narrow slab formed by a projecting corner.

1 75 feet. The slab. About 35 feet up is a good ledge on the right. A move left is then made, and a crack with good holds is climbed to a ledge. The 15 foot wall above leads to another ledge and belay.

2 65 feet. Easier slabs above, finishing with a crack slanting to the left, lead to a large jammed block at the left end of a ledge, which widens to a large grassy shelf (The Oval).

3 65 feet. (Crux). Above the Oval is an obvious crack, formed by the right edge of the Great Flake. Climb diagonally left to the foot of the crack, which is climbed to a large chockstone (running belay). From here, a bold layback leads to good holds on the top of the Flake. (It is also possible to jam this top section of the crack). Pull up on to the horizontal crest of the Flake, and traverse left to a good stance and belay. (It is advantageous to place a runner on the edge of the

Flake to prevent the rope snagging in the crack during the second man's ascent).

4 45 feet. Traverse along the narrow crest of the Flake to a small tower and, after continuing a little way, descend an easy crack to a broad flat ledge (Jeffcoat's Ledge). Belay.

5 60 feet. Walk along the ledge and climb the easy slab almost to the top. Block belay. At the top of the slab is the Cannon; there is a way off at this point.

6 40 feet. Descend a little and make a delicate traverse to the right along a sloping ledge to a small pinnacle leaning out from the wall (running belay). Dropping slightly, continue the traverse (delicate) to a right-angled corner. This is climbed on good holds, first in the corner, then on the outside wall, to a large recess (the V-ledge). The only belay is some distance away at the left extremity of the ledge.

7 65 feet. Climb up the short slab, which bounds the V-Ledge on the right, and, after a difficult step up on to a ledge above, make a slightly ascending delicate traverse to the right across a corner. This leads to an easier-angled slab (junction with Moss Ghyll Grooves), running back to the left with good holds. At the top a large hollow is reached. Belay on the right in a hole, or round a protruding block on the cracked slab above.

8 60 feet. Climb the mossy gully (usually wet) a little way and break out on to a large rock shelf on the left. The steep wall ahead has a delicate start and leads to easy ledges and the summit ridge.

Variation. The Direct Start.
An alternative to pitches 1 and 2. More exposed and harder than the ordinary start. Starts at the point where Rake's Progress meets Moss Ghyll.

1a 65 feet. Start up the corner; then move on to the rib and up to a large stance with an overhanging roof. Belay on a piton to the left. Indifferent natural belay.

2a 75 feet. From the stance, traverse left for 12 feet to a corner, which is ascended with some difficulty. Bearing left all the time, continue up the wall to the Oval. Belay at the foot of the Flake Crack.

Variation. The Direct Finish.

Starts from the belay on the V-Ledge. Good exposed climbing.

7a 90 feet. Follow the ledge to its left end to a small slab. Climb the slab for a few feet and, after a pull-up, continue along some ledges, slightly right, to a gangway. This leads to an overhanging crack with an awkward landing on to a large stance. Belay.

8a 80 feet. The crack (mossy) in the corner leads to easy ledges and the summit ridge.

Variation. The Bayonet-Shaped Crack.

7b 65 feet. Climb up the bounding slab of the V-Ledge and, after making a difficult step up, work back to the left and enter the crack by a very awkward movement. Continue straight ahead up the mossy crack, or chimney to the large hollow at the top of pitch 7.

Variation.

7c 100 feet. Climb over the bounding slab of the V-Ledge and, with a running belay round a knob, descend the bottomless chimney. After about 20 feet it is possible to traverse to the right into a groove (Moss Ghyll Grooves), which is climbed on good holds to the large hollow.

Variation.

35 feet. The small pinnacle mentioned in pitch 6 may be reached directly from Jeffcoat's Ledge by ascending the steep wall, thus short-circuiting pitch 5.

Moss Ghyll Grooves. 260 feet. Severe (hard).
A classic climb of sustained interest. Starts from Moss Ghyll at the top of pitch 3, where a slanting groove runs up the left wall (true right).

1 55 feet. The groove leads to a good ledge, a few yards to the right of the Oval. The overhanging block on the right is then climbed to a grassy corner. Belays on the right.

2 45 feet. Climb 8 feet up the corner and traverse left to a small ledge on the left edge (the Pedestal). Ascend the arête leading back to the groove, which is followed to a stance and belay.

3 20 feet. Continue up the narrowing slab until an easy traverse back to the right into the next groove is possible. Large belay. (The Look-Out).

4 80 feet. The slab ahead is climbed first right, then left, and straight up. Near the top it is necessary to step on to the face on the left once or twice. The recess at the top of the Bayonet-Shaped Crack of Central Buttress is now reached. Belay on the right in a hole, or round a protruding block on the cracked slab above.

5 60 feet. Climb the left wall of the gully for 15 feet and break out to a large ledge on the left. The steep wall above is delicate at its start and leads to the summit ridge.

Variation Start 100 feet. Severe (hard).
An alternative to pitches 1, 2 and 3. Starts at the top of pitch 5 of Moss Ghyll.
100 feet. Traverse left for 15 feet into the groove above that of the normal start. Climb 25 feet to a grass ledge below an overhang. Move to the right into the next groove and ascend it, partly by layback. A running belay can be arranged a few feet

below the point where the slab on the left narrows : a long step is then made across it to the Look-Out (top of pitch 3).

Long Stand. 300 feet. Very severe.

Start as for the Variation Start to Moss Ghyll Grooves.

1 100 feet. Move left over a bulge to gain the next groove above and to the right of Moss Ghyll Grooves. Climb this towards a prominent overhang. Cross the slab below the overhang to its left edge with difficulty, and go up to the overhang. Turn this on the left by a crack, and move up to the stance at the top of pitch 3 of Moss Ghyll Grooves.

2 80 feet. Ascend Moss Ghyll Grooves for a few feet; then move to the right on to a delicate slab. Climb a groove in the slab, until an exposed hand-traverse can be made round the rib on the right into the next groove. Climb the crack in the slab to a recess and thread belay.

3 55 feet. Climb the steep wall and scramble to a block belay.

4 65 feet. Move rightwards, and climb a slabby groove slanting left to the top of Central Buttress.

Last Stand. 300 feet. Extremely severe.

The climb, which is not sustained, takes the crack which falls from the left side of the recess at the top of pitch 1 of Narrow Stand, and is an alternative to that pitch. Starts at the top of pitch 5 of Moss Ghyll and 20 feet below the start of Narrow Stand.

1 100 feet. Climb the steep tapering slab on the left side of the groove until it ends. Move into the crack, which soon becomes narrow, overhanging and awkward. It soon eases, however, and is followed to a ledge with no belay. Use a piton belay or continue.

2 20 feet. The continuation of the crack, which proves much easier, leads to the stance at the top of pitch 1 of Narrow Stand.

3 180 feet. As for Narrow Stand, pitches 2 and 3.

Narrow Stand. 285 feet. Very severe (hard).
Starts up a crack, which splits the groove to the left of Slab and Groove Route.

1 105 feet. Traverse left under the overhang; then climb the crack until it eases (where Slab and Groove enters from the right). Move left to a stance and small belay.

2 60 feet. Climb up past the overhang on to slabs and so to a grass stance and belays.

3 120 feet. Climb the corner on the left (junction with Moss Ghyll Grooves), then right, up broken rocks with pleasant slabs and corners, to the top.

Slab and Groove Route. 240 feet. Very severe.
An excellent climb. Starts up a big slab capped by an overhang on the left-hand side (true right) of Moss Ghyll, opposite Tennis Court Wall.

1 110 feet. Climb the groove on the right-hand side of the slab for 20 feet; then follow a line of holds across to the left into a shallow depression at the foot of a thin crack. Climb the crack until it is possible to step into a pocket near the arête. Follow the edge for a few feet and traverse left into a groove, landing on a small pedestal. A running belay may be arranged on a small flake on the right. Climb the groove until level with a recess on the left; then make a long step right, and go straight up the wall into a corner. Block belay. This corner is immediately above the overhangs that cap the slab.

2 80 feet. Climb the groove above to a stance and belay at its top.

3 50 feet. Easy climbing is followed by a scramble to the top of the crag.

Central Buttress Girdle. 570 feet. Very severe (hard). An excellent climb, which uses some of the best pitches on the buttress. Starts as for Botterill's Slab.

1 50 feet. Pitch 1 of Botterill's Slab.

2 90 feet. Climb pitch 2 of Botterill's Slab to the traverse into the chimney. On gaining the chimney, continue traversing to a ledge in an impending corner. Piton belay.

3 60 feet. Swing out and mantelshelf on to a ledge on the arête on the right. Another awkward move leads to a narrow ledge, which is followed to join Central Buttress at the start of the traverses (top of pitch 5).

4 40 feet. Climb pitch 6 of Central Buttress to the V-ledge.

5 70 feet. Continue along pitch 7 of Central Buttress to the junction with Moss Ghyll Grooves; then descend that climb to a sloping stance and spike belay just above its crux.

6 50 feet. Descend the crux of Moss Ghyll Grooves; then move right to join Long Stand. Climb, delicately, the groove in the slab to the overhang, and hand-traverse to the right into Narrow Stand. Poor stance: it is probably better to continue.

7 30 feet. Descend Narrow Stand to a stance at the top of pitch 1.

8 40 feet. Descend Narrow Stand to a junction with Slab and Groove; climb this to a stance and large flake belays (top of pitch 1 of Slab and Groove).

9 60 feet. Traverse along a narrow sloping ledge on the lip of the overhang, go round a nose and continue along the fault until it ends. Move right, to easier ground, and belay, (junction with pitch 10 of Moss Ghyll).

10 80 feet. The easy slabs lead to the top, (Collie Exit to Moss Ghyll).

Variation. A more logical line, which replaces pitches 7 and 8. 70 feet. Climb Narrow Stand for about 15 feet; then move right, round the arête, and continue the traverse to join pitch 2 of Slab and Groove, which is descended to the stance at the top of pitch 1.

Moss Ghyll. 415 feet. Very difficult (hard).
One of the finest gullies in the Lake District, equally enjoyable in winter conditions. The gully lies between Central and Pisgah Buttresses. The start is below Rake's Progress.

1 30 feet. A chimney with an overhanging chockstone leads to the Progress.

2 40 feet. A rather difficult corner is climbed on the left. Walk into a very deep chimney.

3 40 feet. The chimney. Work out from the back on to the chockstone.
Another short chimney leads to some ledges. Belay.
Pitches 2 and 3 may be avoided by climbing a series of ledges on the right wall.

4 20 feet. A narrow chimney.

5 30 feet. Another chimney.

6 25 feet. Easy slabs lead to a good belay just below the corner on the wall above. A short walk into the gully leads to a recess below Tennis Court Wall.

7 25 feet. The wall. Thread belay in the crack at the right end of the Tennis Court.

8 25 feet. Traverse back to the bed of the Ghyll, and walk up the scree into a large cave. The cave may also be reached by climbing straight up the vertical mossy chimney in the corner, on the left of Tennis Court Wall.

9 10 feet. From the back of the cave climb on to the window sill. Belays.

10 20 feet. Step down and make a short delicate traverse to the left (the Collie Step); then climb easy slabs to a belay in a recess.

11 25 feet. An easy traverse back to the Ghyll, and a large amphitheatre. This may be left in a variety of ways. The various exits are described starting on the left with the Collie Exit and working round to Botterill's Exit.

The Collie Exit. Lies up the sweep of broken slabs on the left.

12 50 feet. The rib in the left-hand corner of the amphitheatre is followed by a crack to some rocky ledges. Block belay.

13 45 feet. The crack above the block is followed by a traverse to the left and the ascent of an easy chimney. Alternatively a traverse at the level of the block leads to the same easy chimney. Ledge and belay.

14 30 feet. The short corner on the left gives on to easy ground.

Barton's Exit.

12a 50 feet. As for the Collie Exit. The rib in the left-hand corner of the Amphitheatre is followed by a crack to some ledges. Block belay.

13a 20 feet. Fairly easy ledges lead to a large grass shelf. Belay.

14a 40 feet. The gully in the corner. It is steep at the start but the angle soon eases. There are good holds but some loose rock. Shelf and belay.

15a 10 feet. A walk to the left followed by an easy chimney.

Collier's Chimney. The deeply-cut chimney on the right.

12b 30 feet. Climb over two chockstones to a belay on the right wall.

13b 25 feet. Back up the chimney and climb through a hole to a stance and thread belay on a boulder. Alternatively the wall on the right of the chimney may be climbed.

14b 40 feet. Traverse out a little and climb over two chockstones. A few feet of scree then lead to a belay. This pitch, though strenuous is not really difficult.
A walk up scree.

15b 35 feet. A rather awkward chimney. Scrambling to the top.

Banner's Exit. 225 feet. Very severe.
Starts up Collier's Chimney.

1 30 feet. As for Collier's Chimney.

2 60 feet. Climb the slab until it steepens; then move left for 20 feet to a stance and piton belay, (top of pitch 1 of Clockwork Orange).

3 110 feet. Climb the left one of three small grooves above the belay to a ledge. Ascend the steep wall leftwards; then go back to the right, to another groove. Climb the groove and a gangway to a grass ledge, (thread and nut belays in the corner on the left).

4 25 feet. Either traverse to the right, along the ledge to finish, or, better, climb pitch 3 of Clockwork Orange.

Botterill's Exit. Starts 20 feet to the right of Collier's Chimney.

12c 35 feet. Step on to a small ledge on the wall and make a short traverse to the right to a crack with good holds. The exit is to the left, after which another traverse right is made to a stance and belay in a crack.

13c 35 feet. The crack is steep at first, but soon eases, and easy ground is reached on the ridge of Pisgah Buttress. Easy-angled slabs lead to the top of the Buttress, or a grass rake leads back to the easy section of Collier's Chimney.

Clockwork Orange. 200 feet. Very severe (hard).

A good climb. Starts at the same point as Collier's Chimney Exit in the amphitheatre of Moss Ghyll.

1 65 feet. Up Collier's Chimney for a few feet until entry can be made on to the impressive slab on the left. Up the slab to a ledge and piton belay.

2 110 feet. As for pitch 3 of Banner's Exit to Moss Ghyll.

3 25 feet. Climb the steep corner to the top.

The Gripe. 190 feet. Very severe (hard).

The climb starts from the top of pitch 8 of Moss Ghyll (below the cave) and ascends grooves to reach the prominent crack-chimney on the right of the huge crevassed block high on the left edge of Pisgah Buttress. A good climb. Difficulties are short and well protected.

1 40 feet. From the bed of the gully move to a ledge on the right below a groove, which is climbed to a good grass ledge on the right. Nut belays in the crack on the right.

2 110 feet. From the right end of the ledge, continue up a groove for 20 feet; then traverse left for 10 feet below a small overhang. (The route crosses pitch 4 of Moses Trod at this point). Break through the overhang and ascend directly to below the steep crack at the right edge of the block. Climb the crack, which widens to a narrow chimney at half height, to the top of the crevassed block.

3 40 feet. Climb the centre of the steep wall behind the crevasse. Scrambling leads to the top of Pisgah Buttress.

Pisgah Buttress Direct. 450 feet. Severe (mild).

Starts about the middle of the face of the buttress at a steep shallow corner. Cairn.

1 80 feet. Climb first a little to the left. About 40 feet up, work right and over an awkward bulge to a little slab, which leads to an easier groove slanting from right to left. The groove is climbed to a ledge and belay.

2 60 feet. Easy ledges on the left, followed by an upward traverse to the right under some doubtful looking blocks, then up a corner to a deep crevasse.

3 25 feet. A staircase corner on the right. Stance and block belay. (Junction with the Girdle Traverse).

4 30 feet. Traverse left along a good ledge to the Fives Court. Thread belay.

5 30 feet. The crack in the corner. Belay.

6 40 feet. Continue up the crack over a bulge to easy slabs, which lead to a large block on the edge of the buttress overlooking Steep Ghyll.

7 10 feet. A difficult pull-up to a ledge with another block belay.

8 50 feet. The ridge above followed by a groove and easier, dirty and mossy rocks. Belay to the right.

9 40 feet. A grassy gully is followed to some slabs.

10 85 feet. Easy-angled slabs.

Variation Start.
80 feet. Round the corner on the right of the direct start is a slab facing Lord's Rake. It is much easier than the direct start, which it joins at the groove above the difficult section.

Variation—Original Route. Very difficult.
Starts from Tennis Court Ledge, reached by ascending Moss Ghyll to the top of pitch 7. The 12 foot crack in the right-hand corner leads to the Fives Court where the direct route is joined. The crack may be avoided by climbing the outside wall on the right of it.

Moses Trod. 470 feet. Severe.
Starts at the right-hand side of the buttress and works up and across to the top of the huge block which is a prominent feature of the left-hand edge of the upper part of the buttress. Starts immediately left of Bos'n's Buttress.

1 60 feet. Climb the rib for 25 feet and then follow an easy groove which slants left to join the top of the first pitch of Pisgah Buttress Direct.
2 50 feet. From the belay ascend directly past jammed blocks to the crevasse (top of pitch 2, Direct Route).
3 60 feet. Straight up for a few feet then traverse diagonally left, crossing the traverse on pitch 4 of the Direct Route, to reach the foot of a flake crack. Climb this to a stance and belay.
4 70 feet. Climb up for a few feet than traverse left on to a rib. Climb this and follow an obvious traverse line left to a perched block. Descend a few feet to belay round this.
5 60 feet. Move up and left from the belay, around the corner overlooking Moss Ghyll and ascend steep rock on good holds until the crack behind the huge block is reached. Follow this to a stance and belays at the top.
6 60 feet. From the top of the block, traverse right immediately under the overhanging nose and climb the rib above to a junction with Pisgah Buttress Direct.
7 110 feet. Finish up Pisgah Buttress Direct.

Bos'n's Buttress. 390 feet. Very severe.
Starts at a chimney at the right edge of Pisgah Buttress and follows a line close to this edge throughout.

1 45 feet. Up the chimney to a stance and belay.
2 45 feet. Climb the steep crack to a grassy stance and belay.

3 40 feet. The wall on the right of the arête is split by a deep chimney. Follow this until a short traverse left leads to a rock ledge and belay.

4 50 feet. Climb the edge for a short way, then make a traverse to the right to the foot of a twisting crack which leads to a stance and belay on the left.

5 25 feet. Climb the slab on the left and the short wall above to a pinnacle belay (junction with Pisgah Buttress Direct).

6 60 feet. Climb the short wall above. Continue up the arête until a move right can be made then climb a steep little wall.

7 125 feet. Finish as for Pisgah Buttress Direct (pitches 9 and 10).

Pisgah Ya Bas. 170 feet. Very severe (hard).
The climb is on the Pisgah Buttress wall of Steep Ghyll, and begins opposite the start of Slingby's Chimney, 10 feet left of the start of Steep Ghyll Grooves. A serious and poorly-protected route.

1 40 feet. Climb an open groove, and at the top, make a high step to the right to finish on a rock ledge.

2 130 feet. Move a few feet to the right, past the stance at the top of pitch 2 of Steep Ghyll Grooves; then climb a short steep wall. Move to the right below a holdless V-groove and climb the steep rib on its right. Move right again, and climb steep rocks and a grassy groove to reach the ridge of Pisgah.

Steep Ghyll Grooves. 185 feet. Very severe (mild).
The climb starts 10 feet right of Pisgah Ya Bas.

1 15 feet. Steep rocks lead to a ledge.

2 20 feet. Climb the wall above to a good ledge and belay.

3 60 feet. Take the easiest line to an open chimney directly above, which is followed to a stance and belay.
4 90 feet. Easier climbing. Start up the groove and finish on the easier upper slabs of Pisgah Buttress.

Steep Ghyll.

This gully divides Pisgah Buttress from the Pinnacle. In summer it is loose earthy and unpleasant, but given good winter conditions, it is transformed into a worthwhile climb of high standard.

Scafell Pinnacle

The Pinnacle has two summits, High Man and Low Man. Most of the routes lead to the Low Man, from which the High Man is reached by the Knife-Edge Arête.

Low Man By The Right Wall of Steep Ghyll. 195 feet.
Severe (mild).

The start is reached by scrambling up the bed of the gully until the walls close in and a mossy chimney is found on the right, level with an unpleasant-looking pitch in the actual bed of the gully.

1 45 feet. The chimney or, more pleasantly, the slabs on its left are climbed to a ledge. Belay. A few feet higher, on another ledge, is a second belay.
2 45 feet. From the right end of the ledge, pull up into the recess above. Continue up the slab on the left on good holds, passing another flat ledge on the right. Grass ledge with belays.
3 35 feet. Pull up on good holds and follow a grass ledge to the left to blocks and a belay.

4 70 feet. Climb over the short grey wall and work to the left on grass ledges until an awkward move leads to a ledge just above the Knife-Edge Arête. On reaching the grass ledge on pitch 3, an easier and quicker alternative is to walk to the right and join Slingsby's Route below the Knife-Edge Arête.

High Man via Steep Ghyll and Slingsby's Chimney
335 feet. Difficult (hard).

An interesting and popular climb. The start is reached by scrambling up Steep Ghyll for about 200 feet until the walls begin to close in. Just below a steep pitch, a series of ledges on the right wall, mark the start of the climb.

1 45 feet. Easy rocks and ledges on the right lead to a terrace.

2 35 feet. Easy slabs above, with a 3-foot step lead to a deep crevasse.

3 20 feet. Step across the crevasse with some difficulty and climb a short slab to a stance and belays at the foot of Slingsby's Chimney.

4 25 feet. The chimney, which is undercut, is awkward to start but has excellent holds. The pitch becomes easier and a recess with a belay on each side is reached.

5 45 feet. The easier continuation of the chimney.

6 55 feet. Easy rocks and scrambling lead to the top of the Low Man. The Knife-Edge Arête is straight ahead.

7 55 feet. The Knife-Edge is ascended. A good stance and belay are found 10 feet further up the Pinnacle.

8 55 feet. Easy climbing leads to High Man.

Variation.

4a 45 feet. Severe. A pleasant variation is to climb the slabs on the left of the chimney and, after about 30 feet, work back to the chimney.

The Waiting Room from The First Pitch in Steep Ghyll 120 feet. Very severe (mild).

The start is reached by scrambling up Steep Ghyll until almost at the top of the first section, where a small cave is seen under the overhanging right wall. On the steep face to the right is a small ledge with a cairn.

1 75 feet. After a long step across the gully, climb the almost vertical rocks into a groove, which leads to some slabs. These are traversed to a good ledge and belay on the right.

2 45 feet. Step round the exposed corner on the right and climb easier rocks to the Waiting Room.

Variation Finish

2a 60 feet. From the belay climb direct up the mossy crack to the left of the stance. It leads to a large ledge below the Crevasse.

The Pinnacle Face from Steep Ghyll. 70 feet. Severe (hard). Starts from the same point as the preceding climb.

70 feet. Make a horizontal traverse right for 30 feet to a V-shaped corner. The step across this is very difficult, but once taken, it is easier to make a diagonal traverse upwards to the right to a belay on the Pinnacle Face, where any of the routes may be joined.

The Pinnacle Face

The front of the Pinnacle proper is supported on a sub-structure of rock, which rises as a wall from the foot of Lord's Rake. The wall is topped by a series of ledges ending on a terrace which stretches from Deep Ghyll on the right to Steep Ghyll on the left. It is from this terrace that the Face climbs start, and one means of reaching it is by the preliminary section of Steep Ghyll. A more direct way is by a breach in the wall a little to the right of a carved cross, where a short incipient gully, widening out after a few feet, ends on the ledges already mentioned.

The Pinnacle Face gives fine slab climbing on rough rock, which dries more quickly than the neighbouring buttresses. It is especially enjoyable in the early evening when the sun has found its way round to this part of the crag. As this is typical slab climbing, many alternative lines are possible. The traditional routes are described in detail and it is left to the individual climber to work out his own variations.

Leftovers. 280 feet. Very severe.

A companion route to Left Edge giving interesting climbing at a reasonable standard. Starts at the same point as Left Edge, in a big corner to the left of Hopkinson's Gully (arrow mark on rock).

1 60 feet. Climb the steep corner for 40 feet (as for Left Edge), and continue straight up to a belay in a grassy nook.

2 75 feet. Climb the groove direct to a grass ledge on the right at the top. Continue up and to the right to arrive in "The Waiting Room". Belay.

3 65 feet. Climb the green crack and its continuation for 30 feet to a ledge overlooking Steep Ghyll. Step right, and traverse into the chimney below the crevasse. Climb this to belay below Slingsby's Chimney.

4 80 feet. Climb the crack to the left of Slingsby's Chimney on to a slab. Climb the slab, with a corner crack on the right, to the top. Move down left; then climb up and to the right to belay on Low Man.

Left Edge. 215 feet. Very severe.
This worthwhile route follows a good line up the face giving steep crack climbing of a type unusual on the Pinnacle. Starts as for Leftovers.

1 100 feet. Climb directly up the steep corner until it is possible to move right, over easier rock, to the foot of an obvious corner. Follow this until a move right can be made to gain the upper edge. Follow easy grass ledges for 15 feet to a small stance overlooking Hopkinson's Gully. Good small belay.

2 60 feet. Straight above is a crack at the side of a huge flake. Climb this and continue up the crack above until a line of good holds can be reached on the right, which leads diagonally left to the Waiting Room.

3 35 feet. The obvious green crack in the back of the Waiting Room leads to an easier groove, which is climbed to the bottom of the Crevasse.

4 20 feet. Follow the chimney to the top of the Crevasse. (Junction with Slingsby's Chimney).

Hopkinson's Gully. 225 feet. Severe (hard).
Starts from the extreme left end of the Pinnacle Terrace. More easily recognised as a shallow corner than a gully and protected at its foot by a 6-foot wall. A little pyramid of rock to its left will help to identify it.

1 35 feet. Climb the short wall, either over the small pyramid of rock, or to the right on good holds. The corner above is followed until a strenuous pull-up leads to a stance and belay.

2 35 feet. The corner ahead leads to a pinnacle reached by going up a flake to the left.

3 40 feet. A thin crack soon leads to a square chimney, which is climbed to a ledge on the right. Belay above and to the left; there is another belay 8 feet above and to the right.

4 30 feet. Continue up the shallow bed of the gully to a block belay, which vibrates slightly.

5 50 feet. Climb straight up the corner until an awkward move is made to the foot of a 16-foot crack, which is followed to a belay at its top.

6 35 feet. The easy chimney above leads to the Crevasse and Slingsby's Chimney.

Jones's Route Direct from Lord's Rake. 215 feet. Severe. A fine traditional route, which starts from the Pinnacle Terrace on the edge of Deep Ghyll.

1 25 feet. An easy slab ends at some detached blocks.

2 50 feet. The Gangway. Climb on to the sloping gangway and traverse to the left. At its end, climb a little more steeply for a few feet, when a horizontal traverse and an easy ascent lead to a niche and small belay on the right (First Nest).

3 25 feet. The wall above is climbed working slightly left on good holds (Second Nest). A flat rock platform is reached. A belay will be found in the crack above the ledge and another one 8 feet above in the corner on the right.

4 50 feet. Step across the shallow gully and follow it for 30 feet to a block, which vibrates. Continue for a few feet and traverse delicately to the left. A short ascent then leads to the Waiting Room. Thread belay 10 feet up the next pitch.

5 30 feet. Climb up into the cave, which has an overhanging roof. At the top, on the right, a triangular ledge projects. This is the Mantelshelf and it is delicate. A standing

position attained, a short traverse along the good ledge (the Toe Traverse) leads to an easier crack, which is followed to a good stance and belay.

6 35 feet. As for Hopkinson's Gully (pitch 6). The chimney above leads easily to the Crevasse and Slingsby's Chimney.

Direct from Lord's Rake to Hopkinson's Cairn. 165 feet. Severe.

Justifiably the most popular route on the Pinnacle Face. Start as for the preceding route.

1 100 feet. As far as the Second Nest the route is precisely the same as the preceding climb (pitches 1, 2 and 3).

2 65 feet. The shallow corner on the right is climbed by the thin crack. Slabs follow and a traverse (with runners at its start) is made past some doubtful flakes to the good flat ledge on the right (Moss Ledge). The steep slab ahead (Herford's Slab) is protected by an undercut base. A small stance in its centre may be reached from either right or left, the latter being easier. From the stance delicate climbing, working into the corner on the right, gives access to magnificent holds and, after a pull-up, Hopkinson's Cairn ledge is easily reached. The only satisfactory belay is reached just before arriving at the ledge. Poor stance.

For a continuation to the summit see Low Man from Hopkinson's Cairn and Jones's Arête from Hopkinson's Cairn.

Moss Ledge Direct. 190 feet. Very severe (mild).

(See Direct from Lord's Rake to Hopkinson's Cairn.) Midway between the starts of Hopkinson's Gully and Hopkinson's Cairn Direct, the Pinnacle Terrace runs over the top of a small buttress. The climb begins at the foot of this buttress.

1 40 feet. The face of the buttress is climbed to the terrace.

2 30 feet. A few feet to the left, a rib on the wall leads, with difficulty, to a ledge. Good holds follow to the First Nest. Belay.

3 120 feet. From the Nest follow a diagonal fault up to the right and round a nose of rock. Slabs with small good holds follow, and lead to some sloping ledges, which are climbed at their right-hand end. The top step is then traversed to the left and Moss Ledge is reached on good holds. There is no satisfactory natural belay on Moss Ledge and Herford's Slab above must be climbed to reach the one below the level of Hopkinson's Cairn Ledge; poor stance.

Right-Hand Edge. 215 feet. Very severe (hard).
The route starts as for Jones's Route Direct from Lord's Rake, and follows the edge between the Pinnacle Face, and the Deep Ghyll wall to Hopkinson's Cairn. A good route with a combination of delicate slab work, and steep, fierce-looking climbing when it ventures on to the Deep Ghyll wall.

1 25 feet. An easy slab (pitch 1 of Jones's Route Direct).

2 50 feet. Follow the gangway for a few feet until it is possible to step on to the slab above. Traverse this diagonally to the right-hand edge. Stance and piton belay.

3 100 feet. Move left under the steep wall and up through a break on to the slab above. Climb this to the right until Deep Ghyll is overlooked. Traverse round the corner on to the wall and ascend diagonally right, up a series of overlaps, until it is possible to move back left to the edge, where the angle eases immediately. Piton belay.

4 40 feet. Climb the slab above to Hopkinson's Cairn.

Low Man from Hopkinson's Cairn. 170 feet. Difficult.

1 40 feet. Start from the left-hand end of the ledge and climb

the corner. At its top, step right and round the corner to a block belay.

2 15 feet. Straight ahead to another belay.

3 15 feet. Climb the wall on the left for a few feet and make a difficult step left to a stance and belay.

4 40 feet. Easy slabs up a slanting gangway. Belays. (The top of Slingsby's Chimney is just to the left).

5 60 feet. An easy chimney followed by scrambling leads to Low Man.

Jones's Arête from Hopkinson's Cairn. 90 feet. Very severe (mild).

1 70 feet. The rocks on the extreme edge of the Pinnacle overlooking Deep Ghyll are climbed to a ledge and belay.

2 20 feet. The Bad Corner. The smooth slab on the right of a corner is climbed from left to right. There are good finishing holds. Alternatively climb directly up the corner on the left. This pitch is exposed. The platform now reached is at the foot of Jones's Arête (pitch 4 of Jones's Route from Deep Ghyll).

Pinnacle Face Direct Finish. 100 feet. Very severe (hard). This provides an excellent continuation to the top of Low Man after ascending the Right-Hand Edge. Starts from the large block on Sansom's Traverse reached by traversing horizontally left from Hopkinson's Cairn.

1 40 feet. From the left edge of the block, climb the grooved wall, delicately, to the edge of the platform under Slingsby's Chimney. Belay.

2 60 feet. Traverse to the right on to a slab. Step up through the overhangs on to another slab, and, from its right-hand end, ascend a very delicate slab to join Low Man from Hopkinson's Cairn.

Edge Hog. 300 feet. Very severe (hard).

This good but serious route takes the line up the gangway-groove fault in the imposing Deep Ghyll wall below Hopkinson's Cairn ledge. Starts 100 feet below the second chockstone in Deep Ghyll.

1 70 feet. Climb the steep wall (protection piton recommended) by way of the flake ledge to gain the gangway. Climb this, surmounting the overhang at the top, and move diagonally right to an awkward stance and piton belay.

2 70 feet. Step left to regain the groove, which is climbed until a step right can be made on to the wall. Climb the wall; then step left to a small ledge. Move up; then make some awkward moves up and left to Hopkinson's Cairn. Belay.

3 90 feet. Traverse to the right to the line of pitch 2, and ascend a corner groove to a flake runner. Traverse to the right, across the wall, and up a shallow groove to a stance and belay below Jones's Arête.

4 70 feet. Traverse right for a few feet to reach a short, shallow, mossy, open corner. Climb this; then move left towards the arête, and pull up a steep wall to a ledge below a steep crack, which is climbed to the top.

Jones's Route from Deep Ghyll. 145 feet. Severe (mild).

The climb runs up a long curving crack cutting into the left wall of Deep Ghyll, and starts just above the top of its second pitch.

1 30 feet. Traverse 10 feet left into the crack and follow it to a stance and belay. Alternatively start 10 feet below the traverse and step almost immediately into the crack.

2 35 feet. The crack, or slabs on its left, are climbed to a niche and slightly loose belay (the Firma Loca).

3 25 feet. A short ascent, and a fairly easy traverse left lead to a spacious ledge and belays just below an arête on the edge of Deep Ghyll.

4 35 feet. Jones's Arête. The left side of its crest is probably the easier. After 20 feet a shelf is reached. The second section is short and involves a hard finger-pull. Belay on a large block.

5 20 feet. An easy crack to the top of Low Man.

Variation Finish—Gibson's Traverse. The last two pitches may be avoided by a short delicate traverse left on to the front of the Pinnacle, to join Low Man from Hopkinson's Cairn.

Variation Finish—Hopkinson and Tribe's Route. Difficult (hard). From the belay at the foot of Jones's Arête (top of pitch 3), descend Bad Corner in the direction of Hopkinson's Cairn to a small ledge, and so make a junction with Low Man from Hopkinson's Cairn at pitch 3. This route is now followed to Low Man.

Variation Finish—Gibson's Chimney. Severe (mild). This is the chimney in the corner on the right of Jones's Arête, and is an alternative to the last two pitches.

4a 65 feet. The chimney is climbed for 40 feet to a good ledge. Traverse left under two large loose blocks, pull up to a shelf and, after a further short traverse left, reach a ledge on the arête near the top. The chimney direct is loose and dangerous.

Slab Climb. 150 feet. Very severe.
Starts midway between Jones's Route from Deep Ghyll and Central Route.

1 80 feet. Climb the steep wall, with some difficulty, to reach the slabs. Follow these to a belay on the left of a pile of blocks.

2 70 feet. Traverse left, and climb with ease, the groove to the right of Gibson's Chimney.

Central Route—Deep Ghyll Slabs. 180 feet. Severe (hard). The climb goes up the slabby wall of the Pinnacle and starts 10 feet to the left of Jones and Collier's climb.

1 60 feet. A short difficult pull-up and a move left are followed by a slab on the right of overhanging rocks. A little overhang is then climbed and Jones and Collier's route is joined and followed to the pile of blocks (top of pitch 1).

2 30 feet. Step on to the steep wall, first left a little, then right, following a depression in the slab to a niche. There is a good hold inside, and another on top of the block which forms the roof of the niche.

3 40 feet. The narrow slab on the face on the right leads to a ledge on Woodhead's Climb (pitch 3a). No satisfactory belay.

4 50 feet. The steep slabs (with small holds far apart) immediately ahead are followed almost to the summit of the Pinnacle. In the last few feet the holds are flaky and unreliable.

Jones and Collier's Climb. 130 feet. Very difficult. The main interest of the climb is the first rather long traverse. Starts at the corner where the Deep Ghyll wall of the Pinnacle is joined by the wall, which runs down from Professor's Chimney.

1 60 feet. Step on to the slab. After a delicate step or two, continue on good holds upwards and to the left of a pile of blocks. Thread belay.

2 35 feet. Continue the traverse left along broken slabs and climb a steep little wall to a large grassy recess.

3 35 feet. The easy grassy corner on the left leads to the top of Low Man.

Woodhead's Climb. 160 feet. Severe (mild).
A good little climb with a fine, exposed finish. Starts at the same place as Jones and Collier's climb.

1 30 feet. Step on to the slab on the Deep Ghyll side and, after a step or two to the left, climb directly up to a good ledge. Pinnacle belay. Alternatively, the steep wall on the right of the corner may be ascended on small holds until it is possible to reach a fine spike and pull into the easy crack leading to the stance.

2 55 feet. Climb on to the wall above from the left end of the ledge, and work to the right to follow the arête to a large grassy recess. Belays.

3 45 feet. Herford's Finish. Climb into a corner on the left and cross the slab above to the right to a small ledge. Continue straight up for a few feet over a bulge and step to the left. A stance and good belay are soon reached.

4 30 feet. An awkward step, followed by easy rocks leads to High Man.

Variation—De Selincourt's Finish. From the small ledge on pitch 3, keep to the right immediately above Professor's Chimney and climb direct to High Man.

Variation. Original Finish. Breaks out left from the grassy recess at the top of pitch 2. Easier than Herford's Finish but less interesting.

3a 35 feet. Traverse round the splintered rocks on the left for 15 feet (cairn). Surmount the bulge above on excellent handholds to a stance with no satisfactory belay.

4a 35 feet. The grassy gully on the right, in which there are some loose blocks, leads to High Man.

Thompson's Route. 110 feet. Difficult.
Starts from the top of the first pitch of Professor's Chimney.

1 40 feet. Descend the chimney for a few feet on its left wall (true right) and traverse outwards and upwards. The angle soon eases and the grassy recess at the top of pitch 2 of Woodhead's Climb is reached.

2 70 feet. As for the Original Finish to Woodhead's Climb (pitches 3a and 4a).

Variation Finish.

2a 55 feet. From the cairn below the bulge (pitch 3a Woodhead's Climb), continue the traverse left for a few feet; then work down a groove, which has a loose block for its lower wall. It is then possible to edge delicately left to a good stance and belay.

3a 15 feet. Descend the easy rocks and grass into the large recess.

4a 35 feet. The crack in the corner leads to Low Man.

Professor's Chimney. 95 feet. Difficult.
Starts high up and on the left of Deep Ghyll. It is the deeply-cut chimney between the Pinnacle and Pisgah leading to Jordan Gap.

N.B. The old Professor's Chimney is the scree-shoot on the right. It has one small boulder pitch.

1 30 feet. A deeply-cut chimney. Good belay 10 feet up on the right wall.

2 35 feet. The easy bed of the chimney. Good thread in the bed of the chimney.

3 30 feet. The steeper continuation. The easier way lies to the right of the dividing rib and back again.

High Man from Jordan Gap. 30 feet. Moderate.
The simplest way up. Starts from a boulder in Jordan Gap, the cleft, which separates the Pinnacle from Pisgah.

A slightly overhanging 10-foot wall to the right from the boulder is climbed, and a traverse to the left is made to an easy trough.

Pisgah from Jordan Gap. 30 feet. Difficult.
A decidely strenuous pitch, which goes direct to the top of Pisgah from the boulder in Jordan Gap.

The Girdle Traverse. About 1,100 feet. Severe (hard).
A splendid expedition in the traditional style. Starts from the top of the first pitch in Professor's Chimney and traverses the whole face of the crag to the top of Collier's Climb. Reversible. The climb is naturally divided into sections: The Pinnacle, Pisgah Buttress, and Central Buttress. The pitches are numbered separately for each section.

Section 1. The Pinnacle.

1 40 feet. Descend the chimney for a few feet on its left wall (true right), and climb the corner for a few feet; then traverse left and upwards to the recess at the top of pitch 2 of Woodhead's Climb.

2 55 feet. Descend pitch 2 of Woodhead's Climb to the pinnacle belay.

3 50 feet. Descend a little, cross a slab and continue along Jones and Collier's Climb to the pile of blocks. Thread belay.

4 45 feet. Descend the staircase below the blocks, with difficulty, for about 15 feet, and continue the traverse to a grassy recess. Poor belays.

5 65 feet. Walk along the grass; then climb a short wall to a grassy slab. At its lower end descend a small cave pitch to easier rocks, which are followed to the excellent belay at the foot of Jones's Arête.

6 25 feet. The Bad Corner. Descend the slab on the edge of the Ghyll and traverse left to a good belay. (The last man may rope down if he wishes).

7 12 feet. Descend a little wall to a large block belay.

8 30 feet. Work down and round the corner and descend a crack to Hopkinson's Cairn Ledge. Belay below the ledge, on Herford's Slab.

9 100 feet. Descend Herford's Slab to Moss Ledge; then traverse horizontally left and make the short ascent to the Waiting Room. Climb the mantleshelf on Jones's Route, and follow the 16-foot crack to the good belay.

Variation—Sansom's Traverse 40 feet

From Hopkinson's Cairn ledge an almost horizontal traverse left leads along good ledges (past a good belay, but poor stance), round an awkward slightly overhanging corner to the top of the 16-foot crack.

10 20 feet. The chimney ahead leads to the Crevasse. Descend the easy slabs into Steep Ghyll and continue down to the level of a conspicuous crack in the wall of Pisgah Buttress.

Section 2. Pisgah Buttress.

1 40 feet. Descend into the corner and cross to the foot of the crack, which is climbed to a good shelf and belays.

2 30 feet. A horizontal widening ledge runs across the face of the buttress. After the first few feet it is possible to join the ledge and walk along it to the Fives Court. Thread belay in the corner crack.

3 12 feet. Descend the slightly overhanging crack in the corner to the Tennis Court. Thread belay. (It is also possible to descend the outer wall and traverse leftwards to the Tennis Court).

4 25 feet. Descend Tennis Court Wall into Moss Ghyll.

Alternative Route from the Fives Court to Moss Ghyll.

a 25 feet. Ascend the grassy crack to a belay.

b 20 feet. Traverse left and upwards, outside and below a detached flake to a large block belay.

c 20 feet. An exposed horizontal traverse is made to the left to a small stance with another doubtful flake.

d 10 feet. A further short traverse leads into Botterill's Exit from Moss Ghyll at a belay.

e 30 feet. Descend the crack and traverse into the Amphitheatre.

f 80 feet. Descend pitches 11, 10, 9, and 8 of Moss Ghyll to the Tennis Court.

5 75 feet. Descend pitches 6, 5, and 4 of Moss Ghyll to the level of a right-angled groove, which cuts into the wall on the left (true right).

Section 3. Central Buttress.

1 30 feet. A charming traverse is followed by a short ascent to a ledge and belay.

2 50 feet. Walk along the ledge, rounding an exposed corner, to the Oval. Thread belay at the foot of the Flake Crack.

3 30 feet. Continue along the narrowing ledge to a jammed block belay at the end.

4 45 feet. Descend the steep slabs, working slightly right under a projecting corner; then step down to the left to a belay on a green shelf.

5 25 feet. Easy ledges lead across to the foot of Botterill's Slab. Block belays. There is also a good belay high up in the crack on the right of the slab.

6 90 feet. Botterill's Slab. (Very severe).
It is usual to finish here and to scramble to the summit up the easy gully of Keswick Brothers' Climb, but the traverse may be continued to near Collier's Climb.

N.B. The 90-foot pitch of Botterill's Slab may be avoided by descending at this point.

Deep Ghyll.—This is the broad and deeply-cut gully, which bounds the Pinnacle on its right. In summer there is very little climbing in it (two short pitches separated by a long walk), but much loose scree, which makes it somewhat dangerous. In winter it is usually a straightforward snow climb but under exceptional ice conditions it can prove an awkward descent.

Deep Ghyll Buttress

Upper Deep Ghyll Buttress. 210 feet. Very severe (mild). The last buttress on the right at the top of Deep Ghyll. A good climb, having the distinction of finishing higher than any other route in England.

1 60 feet. From the foot of a deeply-cut chimney on the left of the main rib of the buttress, overhanging and doubtful rocks are traversed upwards and to the right, to the foot of a groove (runner). The groove has a severe start but becomes easier. A large loose-looking block should be avoided. Shelf with good belays.

2 40 feet. Climb the little wall on the right and follow an easy ascending grooved ledge to a block belay. A large block leans against the wall just above, and the second can climb on to it to hold the leader for the next pitch.

3 50 feet. This pitch offers more interesting climbing than the original one. Start a few feet left of the large block and climb the wall above on good holds until it is necessary to traverse round the rib to the left. An exposed ascent on small holds in a steep shallow groove leads to a good ledge with a doubtful block belay.

4 60 feet. The slab just to the left is climbed for a few feet on small holds and a stride to the right taken into a stone-filled groove, which is followed to the top.

Variations.

1a 50 feet. The deeply-cut chimney, followed by a traverse to the right, may be taken as an easy alternative.

3a 40 feet. The original route. From the belay make a short ascent; then follow a diagonal crack under an overhang to the left. After an awkward move, the good ledge and doubtful block belay are reached.

Upper West Wall Climb. 210 feet. Severe (mild), first pitch only.

The left projecting wall of the Great Chimney. Starts at a groove on the right.

1 40 feet. Climb the groove for 10 feet, slant left delicately and finish up a small corner to a large ledge. Belay. Scramble up to the left-hand corner of the buttress.

2 30 feet. The steep wall is climbed on good holds followed by a short corner.

3 25 feet. An easy groove on the right. Belay.

4 25 feet. The mossy corner on the right is followed by a pleasant upward traverse to the right, and a finely situated ledge with small belay is reached.

5 40 feet. The ridge ahead is climbed for 20 feet; scrambling follows. It is possible to walk off to the right here.

6 50 feet. Two steep corners ahead are climbed and are followed by a 10-foot walk to the left to an easy crack. Scrambling to the top.

The Great Chimney. 50 feet. Very difficult.
This is the obvious, deeply-cut, and wide chimney with a huge chockstone in it to the right of and below Upper Deep Ghyll Buttress. Walk up the bed of the chimney until directly below the chockstone.

1 20 feet. Climb up to a small ledge and belay just under the chockstone.

2 30 feet. Traverse to the right, to a niche below a crack on the right of the chockstone. Follow the crack on to scree.

Jacob's Ladder. 185 feet. Severe (hard).
Starts 15 feet to the right of the foot of the Great Chimney.

1 15 feet. Make a short upward traverse to the right, across the foot of a steep corner, to a belay on the right edge of a ledge.

2 30 feet. Step up the corner, and follow a sloping ledge back to the left; then climb the chimney for a few feet and step left to a small stance on the rib. Belay on the right.

3 20 feet. Climb the vertical crack in the corner.

4 25 feet. Easier rocks on the right are followed by a glacis to the foot of a vertical wall.

5 50 feet. The wall is climbed from near its left side by an upward traverse to the right, to a corner below an overhang. A traverse left is then followed by a difficult entry into a sentry box; good holds then lead to another glacis.

6 45 feet. Climb the steep wall just to the right of the edge.

West Wall Climb. 185 feet. Difficult.
A pleasant climb. Starts about 20 yards down to the right of the Great Chimney.

1 30 feet. A deeply-cut chimney.

2 25 feet. Climb an awkward corner on the right and continue to a ledge.

3 25 feet. The chimney on the left.

4 35 feet. The wide corner ahead has a rib in it. Start on the left and, near the top, cross to the right to reach a ledge.

5 10 feet. Easy rocks are climbed to a ledge below an arête.

6 40 feet. The arête is followed to a large ledge.

7 20 feet. A little chimney, then a small cave pitch.

Grey Bastion. 270 feet. Very severe (mild).
Starts at a cairn just to the right of a prominent projecting corner, which forms the left edge of a high vertical wall opposite Hopkinson's Cairn ledge.

1 35 feet. Climb an incipient crack above the cairn, and continue up a corner to an excellent thread belay. Poor stance. Just on the left there is a good grass ledge with a doubtful block.

2 20 feet. From the grass ledge, climb the steep ridge above, to a stance and belay.

3 50 feet. Climb to the right, up uninteresting broken rocks, to a stance and belay below a steep grey wall, which overlooks a vertical crack.

4 35 feet. The wall is climbed from a smooth ledge on the left by a gangway sloping up to the right (passing a dangerous looking flake) and on to a grass ledge. Now climb a recess to a good belay below an overhanging corner.

5 50 feet. Traverse easy slabs to the right and continue up ledges in the wall above. From the top ledge, which has a block on it, cross a corner on the left to a belay near some blocks in a corner.

6 20 feet. Walk 10 feet left and climb steep rocks to a corner with a pointed flake belay.

7 60 feet. Climb the easy slabs on the right, pull up over the steep wall ahead to a shelf, and follow an interesting crack which leads to the top.

Gobsite. 255 feet. Very severe.
Follows the line of the deep overhanging crack, 40 feet left of Xerxes.

1 40 feet. Climb the rib to a block below the crack.

2 30 feet. Move left into a groove, and climb this to a large pinnacle.

3 50 feet. Traverse to the right, below the overhang, and swing into the crack. Climb this, and easier rock, to a chock belay.

4 35 feet. Climb the groove, delicate in places, and finish up a short crack.

5 100 feet. Climb the short overhanging crack, and easier rock in the same line, to the top.

Xerxes. 240 feet. Very severe (hard).
A good climb on the steep wall of Deep Ghyll Buttress, overlooking Lord's Rake. The face is bounded on the right by grass terraces, and on the left by a prominent wide crack (Gobsite). The climb starts at an obvious V-groove, which leads to a series of discontinuous cracks in the wall above.

1 50 feet. Climb the groove on good but awkwardly placed holds to a ledge with a large block belay, (care is needed with a loose flake near the top).

2 60 feet. Follow the line of the crack up the face behind the belay, via two small ledges, to a sloping grass ledge. Move left to a good ledge with a chockstone belay on the far left.

3 50 feet. From the small corner at the left end of the ledge, climb up a few feet; then follow a line of holds trending right for 10 feet until a mossy scoop (usually wet) is reached. Go up slightly to the left of this to a big terrace.

4 80 feet. Enter the wide gully above at its left side and climb it until an exit can be made on the left to slabs, which lead to the top.

There are several climbs on the crags, which lie to the right (i.e. to the west) of Deep Ghyll Buttress, and above and to the right of Shamrock; these are reached from the path, which leads to Scafell from Lord's Rake (see Topographical).

Castor. 130 feet. Moderate.
Starts 10 feet below and beyond the second col of Lord's Rake, when approached from the foot of Scafell Pinnacle.

1 50 feet. The right-hand edge of the steep ridge is climbed on good holds. Belay.

2 25 feet. The wall ahead is turned on the left, either by a rib or a chimney.

3 15 feet. Easy ridge. Cairn. Scramble to a pile of blocks ahead.

4 40 feet. Climb the wall behind the blocks. The route passes between two very dubious flakes and then goes up a slab to a cairn.

Pollux. 200 feet. Very difficult (hard).
A pleasant climb. Starts about 40 yards down to the right from the second col of Lord's Rake (i.e. to the west), at a prominent pillar projecting from the main mass of rock.

1 25 feet. From the left corner of the pillar traverse upwards into a crack, which is followed to the top. The crack may also be ascended from its foot. Belays.
2 30 feet. Climb the sloping groove on the left to a small stance and belay below a cave.
3 45 feet. Enter the cave and leave by the left wall, which has good holds and leads to a grass shelf with belays.
4 45 feet. The easy rib on the right.
5 55 feet. The prominent rib ahead. Keep to the left for the best climbing.

There are two climbs on Red Ghyll Buttress (206068), the prominent pillar-like buttress rising on the right near the top of Red Ghyll. The buttress is reached either by following Lord's Rake in a westerly direction until it becomes an open scree slope, or by descending the same from where it debouches on the Scafell ridge.

Red Ghyll Wall. 180 feet. Severe (mild).
The climb lies on the left-hand face of Red Ghyll Buttress and starts from a large grassy ledge a few feet to the right of the ghyll. Small cairn.
1 55 feet. Climb a vertical corner with good holds to a narrow shelf; then work left for a short distance to a good rock ledge. The route now goes diagonally upwards to the right to a turf ledge and small belay.
2 25 feet. Climb the left one of two grooves. Stance and good belay.
3 40 feet. Ascend a slab from the left end of a large bilberry shelf. At the top move to the right to a slab with good holds. Small stance and belay.
4 25 feet. Steep rocks with good holds on the left of the face lead to a large recess and belays.
5 35 feet. Climb a slanting crack in an overhanging corner to the top of the crag.

Red Ghyll Buttress. 250 feet. Very difficult.
The start is on the right at a large detached flake and cairn.

1 40 feet. The wall, on the right of a vertical crack, has good holds and leads to a shallow grassy gully.
2 15 feet. Scrambling up to the left.
3 35 feet. The steep wall above is climbed from left to right. The start is very difficult but there are good holds higher up. A large detached flake should be handled with care.
4 35 feet. The corner of the ridge ahead leads to a neck.
5 35 feet. Step across the neck and climb the ridge ahead.
6 90 feet. Pleasant scrambling leads to the top.

The Banister
An easy climb up the ridge on the right of Red Ghyll Buttress. The climb is composed of slabs at a moderate angle.

Scafell Shamrock (205070)

Intermittent Chimneys. 150 feet. Moderate.
A mixed grass and rock route starting on the left side of the Shamrock and about 200 feet below the foot of Lord's Rake. Finishes at the foot of the Third Tower of the Tower Buttress.

Gilt Edge Eliminate. 560 feet. Extremely severe.
A good climb giving strenous and varied climbing. Start 30 feet to the left of Silver Lining, beneath a bulge split by an overhanging groove.

1 60 feet. Ascend the wall below the groove to a recess (thread runner); then bridge the groove to a good hand-hold high on the right. Stride left; then go straight up to a small ledge. Piton belay.
2 25 feet. Move right to a crack; climb it, and traverse to the right to a ledge and thread belay.
3 75 feet. Ascend the short chimney. Continue up a rib until a move right leads to a stance below a thin crack, (flake and nut belays).

4 50 feet. Climb the crack, moving right at the fork. It then bulges slightly. Layback up until some awkward moves can be made straight up to a small stance. Piton belay.

5 80 feet. Move diagonally left until a series of cracks leads to easy ground, (part of pitch 5 of Silver Lining).

6 100 feet. From the left end of the ledge, climb the wall to a small overhang. Surmount this and move left to the edge. Move round, and up overhanging rock until a step right leads to a short gangway. Go up this to the foot of a thin overhanging crack, which is climbed to large block belays.

7 100 feet. Easy ground leads to the foot of the final wall.

8 70 feet. In the centre of the wall just left of a thin crack is a series of bulges. Layback the first to a good hold on the left; then climb straight up to a good ledge, trend left, and up to the top.

Silver Lining. 415 feet. Very severe.
A good direct climb with less difficulty than its appearance would suggest. Starts just to the left of the Tower Buttress; the first pitch takes the parallel slanting chimney to the left of the Tower Buttress.

1 50 feet. Climb broken rocks to the left of the chimney; then trend right, and back diagonally left, to stance and belay at the foot of the chimney.

2 65 feet. Follow the chimney until it gives out; then traverse delicately right, to a junction with the Tower Buttress.

3 75 feet. Ascend a few feet up the chimney, before moving right on to a rib, which is followed to grass ledges and a large block belay at the left side of the buttress.

4 65 feet. Descend diagonally right, until a traverse can be made across the face into a steep crack (junction with Shamrock Buttress). Climb this, bearing left at the top, to a stance and large belay.

5 80 feet. Follow a steep slab diagonally left for 20 feet; then move left again for a few feet, and follow the crack up to a large grassy terrace.

6 80 feet. A large overhanging rib lies above. Start directly below this, and climb up into the corner below the roof until it is possible to swing right, on very good holds, on to the rib. Climb the steep rock straight ahead on good holds to the platform at the top of pitch 10 of the Tower Buttress.

Finish up the Tower Buttress.

The Tower Buttress. 690 feet. Severe (hard).
The start, below a wide deeply-cut chimney, is almost opposite the large boulder at the top of Hollow Stones.

1 50 feet. A grassy chimney is climbed on good holds, mostly up its left-hand edge. The exit may be made on the right or up a scoop on the left. Large flake belay.

2 10 feet. An upward traverse is made to the right into a chimney. Belay.

3 25 feet. The chimney is followed by steep grass and leads to a nook and belays.

4 60 feet. The steep wall above the belay is climbed with some difficulty, moving slightly left near the top, to a good flat ledge. A narrow slanting chimney follows to a grass ledge and belay.

5 40 feet. The wide easy chimney ahead.

6 30 feet. The chimney to a terrace and belay.

7 40 feet. Continue up the chimney; exit on the left.

8 35 feet. Grass in the right corner, followed by a chimney, leads to a wide terrace at the foot of a wall.

9 40 feet. A ledge, slanting up to the right, gives a delicate traverse to a block belay on the corner.

10 70 feet. Step left from the belay; then climb the wall over protruding blocks to a ledge. Traverse left to a roofed sloping slab, grass covered at its foot (the Gallery). Continue along under the overhang, rounding a corner, where a foothold on the face is the key. The vertical rocks above can be climbed, but it is easier to continue a little way to where the wall is less steep. A platform is reached with belays and a cairn.

11 100 feet. Scrambling over boulders leads to the foot of the Third Tower.

12 80 feet. The Tower is turned by descending rightwards by easy slabs, then climbing a narrow chimney. Care is required on account of loose blocks. Traverse round to the right to a grass nook and block belay.

13 50 feet. The ridge on the right. Step left at the finish and climb the buttress above, either by a chimney or a slab on the right, to a grass shelf with large blocks.

14 60 feet. From the left end of the blocks, climb the wall above. Continue up the ridge a little way and finish up a short chimney.

A short scramble, followed by a walk along a horizontal ridge, leads to the foot of the summit tower of the Shamrock and to Lord's Rake.

Variation.

12a 35 feet. Very severe. The central one of three cracks is climbed, beginning 30 feet down to the right from the highest point of the ledge. Work up right for 15 feet to a large spike runner. Bear left, and climb the steep crack by strenuous jamming.

Shamrock Buttress. 350 feet. Very severe.
Starts about 50 feet down the scree to the right of the Tower Buttress in a grassy corner below an open chimney. The route

traverses left on to the main rib, which overhangs the base of the crag, and then follows an open chimney, which runs up from the overhangs. It then carries on directly up the face in the line of the chimney, which soon becomes a crack.

1 80 feet. Up the open chimney, working left as soon as possible, over grass ledges to a belay near the edge of the overhang. A harder but more pleasant alternative is to start up the overhanging wall a little to the left of the open chimney, and then traverse to the right along a ledge to make an entry into the chimney.

2 110 feet. Traverse left for 10 feet, down the grass ledge, and step on to the good rib, which overhangs the foot of the crag. Climb this, keeping close to the edge, until a bottomless open chimney is reached. Climb this to the end of a terrace. Small belay.

3 80 feet. The steep wall above is climbed up the cracks immediately above the belay, a large block being passed on the left. Stance in a crevasse behind the block ; belay.

4 80 feet. From the top of the block climb up for a few feet before stepping right, on to the top of the overhanging nose. The rib soon leads to easy rock and grass ledges, which are followed to a large terrace at the top of pitch 8 of the Tower Buttress. Large block belay inset in the terrace.
Finish up the Tower Buttress.

The Rampart. 270 feet. Severe (hard).
Dirtier and less interesting than the Tower Buttress. Starts at about the same point as Shamrock Buttress in a grassy corner below a groove.

1 25 feet. Climb the vertical rocks on the immediate right of the green groove, and make an awkward traverse to the right to reach a good shelf and belay.

2 15 feet. Make a sensational traverse round the projecting wall on the right. A short ascent then leads to a grassy corner. Poor belay.

3 60 feet. Traverse the slab on the left of the corner on an ascending line of holds. Now cross, horizontally, the face on the left, to a grassy gully and block belay.

4 25 feet. Climb the dirty awkward corner to a projecting belay just below a rock ledge at the foot of a steep groove.

5 40 feet. Enter the groove by an upward move from the left and climb, with difficulty, until an exit can be made to the right. (Loose blocks). A belay can be arranged round the sloping shelf.

6 45 feet. Climb easier rocks, leading left, to a flake belay below an obvious cave.

7 60 feet. Traverse into the cave on the right; then cross to the left on a sloping shelf. Continue across the face to the left, and to easier rocks, which lead to a grass terrace below pitch 9 of the Tower Buttress.
Finish up the Tower Buttress.

BLACK CRAG (201070)

This is the large mass of rock seen on the right from near the top of Brown Tongue. In spite of its grassy appearance it yields several routes, and is sometimes climbable when the main crags are definitely out of condition. The quality of the climbing is, however, in no way comparable with Scafell proper.

Sinister Ridge. 390 feet. Very difficult (hard).
Starts at a cairn on a grass ledge in a little bay, just to the right of the lowest point of the left-hand ridge.

1 30 feet. Climb the broken slab to a grass shelf with belay.

2 20 feet. Easy rocks are climbed to the foot of a V-groove. Belay.

3 65 feet. The climb goes up on the right of the groove, crosses left at its top and up steep rocks, trending slightly right again, to a ledge and belay. 25 feet higher over grass is a notch belay on the left of a corner.

4 20 feet. The crack in the right wall of the corner is climbed. The rocks have an awkward tilt and are very mossy and dirty. Belay.

5 35 feet. The grey wall above is climbed on small good holds, starting at a leaning flake. Belay.

6 35 feet. Step round the corner on the right by a grass ledge and climb the steep wall on good holds. Belay. About 12 feet higher, on another ledge at the foot of a steep wall, there is another belay.

7 40 feet. Step on to the wall towards its right end and gain the arête. After a few feet, a groove is followed upwards to the left, past some loose blocks, to a right-angled corner with a pointed jammed block belay.

8 25 feet. Climb the 10-foot wall on the left of the corner and continue horizontally along grass ledges to a shallow gully.

9 15 feet. The ridge on the left is reached by a slanting shelf. Small belay.

10 40 feet. The steep ridge is climbed, with some difficulty, to a grass ledge and large flake belay. It is easier to climb the shallow gully on the left of the ridge.

11 65 feet. A steep and difficult groove in front is climbed for 25 feet. The slabs on the right of the corner are then followed up to the right finishing back left. Grass ledges and scrambling lead to the shoulder of the crag.

Geodesic. 275 feet. Very severe (hard).
Start at the same point as Plumb Line.

1 110 feet. Climb the left-hand groove to a flake on the arête on the left. Traverse left below the overhang, and regain the arête above it at a small ledge. Climb straight up on good holds; then trend slightly left to a narrow ledge, (nut belays).
2 45 feet. Climb the thin crack above until it peters out; then go up a steepening slab on the left to a ledge. Belay.
3 60 feet. Pull up a short wall to another ledge. Move up and traverse left across the steep, open groove to a good foothold. Climb the groove, finishing with difficulty on a large grassy ledge, (poor belays).
4 60 feet. The arête on the left leads to the top.

Plumb Line. 280 feet. Very severe (mild).
The route follows a series of grooves in an almost direct line to the summit of the crag, and crosses the Diagonal Route at the grassy groove on pitch 3. Starts at a cairn below a black groove in a patch of light-coloured rock to the left of the Diagonal Route. The groove is approached by way of a few feet of very steep grass.

1 60 feet. Enter the groove from the left and climb to where it forks (good spike). The left-hand crack is then followed to a nook in the grassy groove. Belay. (Touches Diagonal Route here).
2 60 feet. Climb the grassy groove ahead to a niche. Thread belay high in the crack.
3 100 feet. Climb the crack until it is possible to step left to a small rock ledge at the foot of a short steep mossy wall. This finishes with an awkward movement to a grassy corner. Now follow a fault with a thin crack in

it to another grassy corner with some insecure-looking flakes. Follow the grassy grooves above until a delicate slab leads to a ledge on the left with a fine belay.

4 60 feet. Climb the wall above the belay to the foot of a steep crack which is followed to the finish.

The Diagonal Route. 355 feet. Very severe (mild).
As seen from the top of Brown Tongue, the route follows a line from a corner on the right of the main face and goes diagonally upwards to the left, under a big overhang, and then underneath a prominent green corner. A grassy climb, rather lacking in character, best climbed after a few dry days. Starts up a slab below some dark rocks just to the left of the prominent corner.

1 50 feet. Climb the slab, first slightly left, then right to a good belay and poor stance.

2 35 feet. Continue over grassy slabs to a large hyacinth-filled recess. Good thread belay in the corner-crack, rather difficult to arrange.

3 100 feet. In order to attain the main rib 20 feet to the left, first traverse from the corner across a large flake and grass ledges; then descend the groove to reach the rib. Follow the rib to an obvious traverse rising to the left. A short delicate ascent is then made to a grass ledge, often damp. Belay on a perched block or around a small chockstone in the crack above.

4 55 feet. From the grass ledge, traverse left to the blocks on the skyline and then move up and across to a grass shelf. Belay. Walk along the shelf to a corner.

5 50 feet. Climb 10 feet to a higher ledge and go to a point from which to start the left wall. Climb this to the large flake belay at the foot of the last pitch of Sinister Ridge.

6 65 feet. The last pitch of Sinister Ridge.

Variation Finish 90 feet. Goes up the large open corner above the start of pitch 5. Climb the left wall of the corner for a short distance, and then follow the corner-crack to a cave. Move out on to the left wall, when easier climbing leads to the top.

Dexter Slab. 185 feet. Very difficult (hard).
The climb lies up the slabs on the left of a wide easy gully bounding the buttress on its right. It starts at a cairn at the foot of a series of projecting slabs.

1 50 feet. The left-hand edge of the first slab is climbed to a ledge with a doubtful thread belay.
2 15 feet. Traverse to the right, to a good belay on the wall on the left of some blocks.
3 60 feet. Climb the blocks and move a little to the left before continuing up the wall above. About 40 feet up there is a very awkward stretch of 10 feet; then good holds give on to a small stance and belay.
4 40 feet. Traverse upwards and to the right to a belay on the edge of the gully and a terrace running back to the left.
5 20 feet. Walk along the terrace and climb the wall above the middle. Belay. Simple scrambling follows.

Variation Start. The wall on pitch 3 can be reached by first climbing the white slabs to the right of the original start.

Saxifrage Ridge. 200 feet. Very severe.
The climb takes a direct line up the crag, finishing on the left of a prominent corner. Start as for Shelob, at the lowest point of the buttress at the junction of the two western gullies.

1 40 feet. Climb the nose on the left of Shelob, and continue left over a series of overlaps to a belay in a grassy corner.
2 80 feet. Climb the narrow crack in the right wall of the corner for 25 feet, by-passing the overhang, to a ledge. Move left into the corner and climb it to a piton belay.

3 80 feet. Step left below the overhangs on to a ridge and climb this until it meets a steep wall. Climb the wall, keeping left of the corner, to the top.

Shelob. 220 feet. Very severe.
Starts as for Saxifrage Ridge.

1 60 feet. Ascend a steep shallow groove to a grass ledge. Step right to loose blocks. Piton belay.

2 70 feet. Climb the groove above marked by a rock scar on the right. Bear right up grass and climb the wall. Belay on a grass ledge on the left.

3 90 feet. Traverse right and climb straight up the steep wall.

The Mousetrap. 190 feet. Very severe (hard).
A serious route, lacking in line but not in difficulty. Start 20 feet left of Hole and Corner Gully (cairn) below a rowan.

1 60 feet. Climb up to the rowan and go diagonally left to a grass ledge on the arête below the obvious corner. Small stance and block belay.

2 130 feet. Climb the corner and slab on its left, until it is possible to climb the right wall; then follow a diagonal line across grooved rock, over a hollow block at the foot of a corner. Continue the traverse to a rib. Climb the rib and vegetation-filled grooves to the left of the overhangs. Step right, and continue direct to the top.

Hole and Corner Gully. Moderate.
This runs up at right angles to the wide easy gully mentioned in Dexter Slab route. It is about 150 feet long, but has only three short pitches.

CLIMBS ON SCAFELL EAST OF MICKLEDORE

Broad Stand. Moderate.

This is the shortest way on to Scafell from Mickledore and the usual way down from climbs in the vicinity. The start is about 25 yards down the scree to the left (east) of Mickledore. A deep cleft is entered then a corner on the left is climbed, and a little crack leads to a large ledge below the step, 9 feet high. This may be climbed on the left up the wall, or in the corner; both are awkward. A few easy ledges follow, and well-marked track leads to the ridge of the mountain.

Mickledore Chimney. 250 feet. Moderate (direct finish difficult). Beware of stones kicked down from Broad Stand.

Continuing down the scree from Broad Stand, this is the deeply-cut chimney bounding the East Buttress on the right. Scrambling leads to a large chockstone. The usual exit is up the short awkward wall on the right. The direct finish goes past the chockstone on the left to a stance and belay below the double chockstone pitch. The chimney is climbed to a ledge on the left wall (15 feet), then go up the right-hand corner (20 feet). Walk up scree (100 feet) to a chimney on the right which is followed by a short traverse out to the right.

THE EAST BUTTRESS (210069)

The East Buttress is essentially a climbing ground for the proficient since, with only one exception, the routes are in the very severe grade. Seen from Mickledore, its apparently continuous overhangs, extensive patches of wet rock and northerly aspect, give it a most formidable appearance. Furthermore, since the earlier routes tend to follow the natural drainage courses, the crag has acquired something of a 'rogue' reputation.

The south-east face, however, is not at all like this and may be in sunlight all morning, drying quickly. The buttress has the added advantage that, by making an early start, it is possible to enjoy a climb in the morning sunshine while Scafell crag is still in shadow.

The normal way off the East Buttress is by striking right about 60 feet above the top of Mickledore Grooves and, after descending into and crossing the upper part of Mickledore Chimney, Broad Stand can be followed down to Mickledore. From the south-east face it is easier to traverse around the left end of the crag in order to descend to the terrace at the foot of the face.

With the exception of the first four climbs starting from Mickledore Chimney, the routes are described from right to left.

About 80 feet up Mickledore Chimney the left bounding wall rises steeply beyond a large slab. There are four climbs on this wall, three of which follow a series of parallel cracks. Although short and not characteristic of the East Buttress, they provide interesting problems. The routes are described in the order they are reached when ascending Mickledore Chimney. The starts of these climbs are sometimes subjected to bombardment by rocks kicked into Mickledore Chimney by hikers descending Broad Stand. Take a sheltered stance at the foot of the climbs.

Pernod. 180 feet. Very severe.
The left edge of the wall forms an arête above the slab. A splendid little climb, which follows this arête and the wall above, to give the best of these routes.

1 60 feet. Climb the corner on the right of the large slab for about 20 feet, when it is possible, by a strenuous move, to traverse to the right, on to the arête, which is climbed to a ledge and piton belay.

2 120 feet. From the right-hand end of the ledge, climb an obvious thin crack past a detached block. After 20 feet the angle eases and easy climbing leads to the top.

Variation. Direct Finish. 100 feet. Very severe (hard).

2a 100 feet. Climb the steep corner behind the belay, in two sections, until it finishes. Easy climbing then leads to the top.

Tia Maria. 140 feet. Very severe.

The climb follows the left one of two cracks, which run up the wall to the right of Pernod. It starts 10 feet to the right of and above Pernod.

1 40 feet. The crack is followed to a small stance and thread belay; the slight overhang at 15 feet is the hardest part of the climb.

2 50 feet. Continue up the crack to a recess.

3 50 feet. Climb the crack running from the left-hand corner of the recess to the top.

Tio Pepe. 140 feet. Very severe.

The route, which climbs the crack parallel to Tia Maria on its right, goes to a chockstone belay in a corner.

Absinthe. 145 feet. Very severe (mild).

The climb runs up the wall just to the right of Tio Pepe, and starts from the top of a rock step in Mickledore Chimney.

1 40 feet. The wall is climbed on good holds to a grass ledge. Belay.

2 30 feet. Move along to the right-hand end of the ledge, which slopes down from right to left, and step on to the wall above. Climb diagonally left to a small rock stance with hook belay on the wall above.

3 75 feet. Climb the steepening wall, tending rightwards towards the triangular overhang above, and then finish up a crack on the immediate left of the overhang. Huge block belays.

Chartreuse. 220 feet. Very severe (hard).

A good route, with a sudden transition from delicate to strenuous climbing, which follows a line near the left-hand edge of the large slab bounding the groove of Mickledore Grooves on the left. Starts from a point about 50 feet up Mickledore Chimney, and follows an obvious ledge running to the left (some 20 feet lower than the stance and belay at the top of pitch 1 of Barry's Traverse, the variation start to Mickledore Grooves).

1 90 feet. Move along the ledge to the left until a delicate traverse is necessary to attain the bottom of a shallow right-angled groove running straight up the face. Follow the groove directly to a stance and belay at the top of pitch 2 of Mickledore Grooves.

2 100 feet. Move round the corner on the right and up to a small rock ledge. Move slightly left; then follow a diagonal crack up to the right and surmount the bulge (as for Mickledore Grooves). Move back immediately left and up, when delicate climbing leads to a resting place on the left of a huge block. Traverse to the right, under the block, to the bottom of the deeply-cut crack and climb this (strenuous). Stance and perched block belay.

2a The resting place on the left of the huge block may also be reached by ascending the crack immediately behind the stance at the top of pitch 2 of Mickledore Buttress, the obvious square roof being passed on the right.

3 30 feet. Easy climbing ahead and up the crack to the finish.

The Fulcrum. 180 feet. Very severe.

A pleasant climb, which winds its way through an area of steep rock. Start about 40 feet left of Mickledore Chimney at the first break in the wall.

1 50 feet. Climb up for 15 feet until a groove on the right can be entered. Climb the groove to where Mickledore Grooves crosses, (small stance and nut belay).

2 60 feet. Ascend the recessed wall on the left to a slab. Traverse left across the slab, under an overhang, to enter the base of a groove. Climb the groove to small stance and piton belay.

3 70 feet. Continue up the groove to the overhang and take the steep crack on the left. Pull out to the right at the top; then move left to an arête and go up to the top.

Mickledore Grooves. 225 feet. Very severe.

This classic of the district, which gives sustained delicate climbing, starts about 25 feet to the left of The Fulcrum at the foot of a rightward-slanting gangway.

1 30 feet. A little overhanging wall is climbed by a stiff pull-up; then the slab on the right is ascended to a stance and small belay at the foot of two grooves.

2 55 feet. The left-hand groove is climbed for 15 feet and a difficult step is then taken into the big right-hand groove; its bed is followed to a grass ledge with a large block belay.

3 140 feet. Step on to a ledge on the face of the slab to the right. (A belay may be taken here thereby reducing the run-out to 120 feet). After stepping left, follow a diagonal crack to the right; there are good holds to overcome the overhang. The next objective is a groove away up on the right. The large mass forming its right wall is undercut at the level of the foot of the groove. Delightful balance climbing up the groove follows.

Just before the groove steepens, a traverse to the right can be made to a sloping ledge and so around the corner on the right. Continue horizontally for about 30 feet, when a mossy opening in the wall above leads to the top of the climb. By walking back to the left, a stance and belay can be found above the groove.

Variation. Direct Finish.

20 feet. Instead of the step right from the final groove, continue straight up, with difficulty, until stopped by the final overhanging corner; then go to the left and up to the top.

Variation. The Slab Start (Barry's Traverse).
This alternative to pitches 1 and 2 of Mickledore Grooves joins the original route at the ledge where the final pitch emerges on to the slab. The ledge is reached by a rising traverse from the extreme right-hand edge of the great slab. The first pitch is merely a scramble but the second is rather more difficult than the original start.

1a 70 feet. Beginning at the foot of Mickledore Chimney and keeping just to the left of it, a scramble follows the right-hand edge of the slab until it is terminated by a steep wall. Stance and belay.

2a 40 feet. A delicate rising traverse leftwards across the slab leads to a ledge and the original route.

Leverage. 160 feet. Extremely severe.
A few feet to the right of the start of Mickledore Grooves, a line of thin cracks runs up the wall above. The route has a deceptively scrappy appearance from below, but gives good sustained climbing, with ample protection.

1 75 feet. Climb the line of the cracks; then move to the right on to a slab. Traverse left directly on to the bulge. Climb this (strenuous and awkward) and follow the line of cracks up steep rock, past a second bulge, to the main bulge, which is the crux. When a landing can be effected above this, the angle very soon relents, and easier climbing up a chimney-groove leads to a stance, (piton or nut belays).

2 85 feet. Climb the groove above the stance; then move to the right, into the corner. Climb the corner to the obvious square roof, traverse under it, and up to make an awkward landing on the slab on the right. Continue up steep rock to a stance and belay.

Dyad†. 210 feet. Extremely severe.

A difficult and strenuous climb, which at present uses some artificial aids. Starts 15 feet left of Mickledore Grooves and follows a thin crack up the wall above.

1 45 feet. Climb the steep ramp (resting on nuts as required) until it is possible to pull out to the right on good holds. Climb the crack for a further 15 feet to a poor stance and piton belay.

2 25 feet. Move up to the right for a few feet to the base of a thin crack, which is climbed using a nut for aid. Mantleshelf up at the top, and move left to a large ledge. Piton belay.

3 60 feet. Move up to the foot of the groove above, and climb it until it is necessary to gain the rib on the right. Climb the rib for 10 feet; then step left on to the base of a slab, which is climbed to a grass ledge and belay.

4 80 feet. Climb the crack to the right of the belay, (pitch 4a of May Day Direct Finish).

† This route has not been checked by the guide writers.

May Day Climb. 275 feet. Very severe (hard).

An interesting route with a rather strenuous start but very pleasant upper pitches. Pitons are in place on the initial slab to safeguard the leader. The route starts up the slab in a corner about 20 feet to the left of Mickledore Grooves (20 feet to the right of Overhanging Wall).

1 60 feet. Climb the slab to a sloping 3-inch ledge 15 feet up. Continue up the slab, which entails strenuous climbing; then traverse round to the right for some 25 feet. Piton belay and awkward stance.

2 50 feet. Ascend the ferocious-looking scoop, which overhangs slightly at its start. (Small but sufficient finger holds come to light when most needed). Now traverse the slab to a thread belay in a corner. Friction stance. (It may be found more convenient to combine pitches 1 and 2 into one run-out).

3 40 feet. Traverse to the left round an overhanging corner and ascend the slab to a corner and belays.

4 25 feet. From the left corner ascend the crack, by jamming, to a belay at its top.

5 20 feet. Climb the scoop directly above the belay, on good holds, to a belay (line only) at the foot of the slab.

6 80 feet. Climb the mossy slabs to the finish.

Variation. **Direct Finish.** 160 feet. Very severe (hard).
The steep corner above pitch 2 makes an interesting variation on the rare occasions when it is dry. More difficult than the usual finish, and two slings and one piton are normally used for aid.

3a 80 feet. From the friction stance, move straight up the crack above the belay and enter the corner on the right. Climb the corner to a piton below the final steep crack. From a foothold above the piton, a good handhold can be reached on the right wall and a traverse made to the arête. Continue up easy ground to a grass ledge and belay. Alternatively the crack above the piton may be taken direct.

4a 80 feet. Climb the wide crack behind a holly for 40 feet and finish up easy rock.

Overhanging Wall. 225 feet. Very severe.
The route starts about 20 feet down to the left of May Day Climb at a ledge, which is heavily overhung and on which are two large boulders.

1 15 feet. Climb the awkward corner to the left of the ledge to a good stance. Belay up to the left.

2 35 feet. Ascend about 3 feet and traverse delicately to the right and upwards to a rib; descend on the right of it and, after a long stride, climb a difficult crack with the aid of a piton (in place). Small stance with a movable but mechanically sound belay.

3 35 feet. Swing round into a crack on the right and climb over a bulge. Ascend a few feet until it is possible to traverse to the right and, after a pull-up, reach a good resting place. Traverse a slab leftwards (avoiding some loose blocks), work into a corner and climb out to a good grass stance and belay. White Slab Variation starts from here. (Pitches 2 and 3 may be combined to avoid an awkward stance).

4 45 feet. Step into a recess on the right and climb up the bed of a corner to a good belay.

5 45 feet. Continue up the corner, which is steep at first. Small belay.

6 50 feet. A vertical chimney. After about 20 feet the climbing becomes easier and leads to a good belay just at the top of the chimney.

Variation Finish. The White Slab. 120 feet.
Although traditionally known as a variation, the White Slab is now the usual finish to the route giving finer climbing than the original. Starts from the belay above pitch 3 of Overhanging Wall.

4a 20 feet. From the stance, traverse left to a grass ledge at the foot of the great White Slab.

5a 50 feet. Climb the slab to a large square block in its centre. Belay round the block.

6a 50 feet. Go straight up from the top of the block, on small holds, to a good ledge. Start at the right-hand end of the ledge and work leftwards. This pitch is usually wet.

Minotaur. 250 feet. Extremely severe.
An excellent climb with difficult and varied situations. Start as for Overhanging Wall.

1 80 feet. Start up Overhanging Wall, and after stepping right on to the large rib, move straight up to a scoop. Follow a white slab up to the left, and from the top of this make an awkward step up, over the bulge above, and so reach the foot of The White Slab. Belay.

2 80 feet. Climb The White Slab for 20 feet until a move up and right can be made on to a big gangway, which is followed almost to its top. Spike belay.

3 50 feet. Climb to the end of the gangway, and ascend the corner to a slab on the left (wet). Climb this, and exit on the left to a grassy ledge.

4 40 feet. Go diagonally left up another slab; then scrambling leads to the top.

Moonday. 280 feet. Very severe (hard).
A good route, which breaks through the bulging wall to the left of Overhanging Wall but marred somewhat by the cascades of water which usually protect it. The climb starts at the lowest point of the easy-angled slab to the left of and below the start of Overhanging Wall.

1 45 feet. Climb the slab until a step to the right can be made on to the ledge stance above pitch 1 of Overhanging Wall.

2 25 feet. Climb the bulging wall above until an awkward move to the left can be made to the grass ledge below an overhanging groove. Piton belay.

3 40 feet. From the ledge, mount a block on the left from which a piton (in place) above the bulge can be reached. Pull over, and climb the slab above to the large ledge below the White Slab.

4 120 feet. Follow the right-hand side of the White Slab for a few feet until a light-coloured slab leads off to the right. Go up this to the stance below the final chimney of Overhanging Wall.

5 50 feet. Pitch 6 of Overhanging Wall. The chimney is climbed to the top.

Variation. The Doomwatch finish.
Starts 100 feet up pitch 4, (piton belay) and climbs the ragged crack in the wall on the left, giving difficult if pointless climbing.

5a 90 feet. Move up to the foot of the very steep crack. Climb it, strenuously, and exit left on to a glacis at the top. From the glacis climb the corner, or the arête on the right, to the top of the crag.

Armageddon. 270 feet. Very severe (hard).
A steep and serious climb, which follows a diagonal line leftwards from the foot of Overhanging Wall. A competent last man is essential. The start is as for Moonday.

1 45 feet. Pitch 1 of Moonday.

2 25 feet. Pitch 2 of Moonday.

3 25 feet. Make for an obvious ledge on the left, aided by a rope through the piton above the bulge on Pitch 3 of Moonday. Poor belay.

4 25 feet. Ascend 10 feet and traverse delicately left to the foot of a 15-foot crack. Poor stance and piton belay.

5 20 feet. A sound piton can be placed high in the crack, an indifferent piton being necessary to reach it. Finish the crack by a short layback. Inserted chockstone belay.

6 80 feet. Make an exposed balance move round the corner to the left. Climb the slab past a good ledge; then go straight up to a stance and poor belays below a wide corner-crack.

7 50 feet. Pitches 7 and 8 of Great Eastern Route.

The Centaur. 315 feet. Very severe (hard).

A splendid solution to the problems of the main buttress of the crag formed by the junction of its north-east and east faces. Although the difficulty is nowhere excessive, the standard is sustained and the route has a serious nature. One of the best climbs on the East Buttress. The route starts in the groove immediately to the right of the start of Great Eastern Route.

1 60 feet. Climb the groove directly above the start of Great Eastern Route on good holds, passing a good ledge on the right, to a stance. Piton or thread belay.

2 45 feet. Climb the corner for 10 feet; then move out left on to the edge. Follow the edge for 15 feet until an obvious line of holds leads back to the right across the groove to a stance. Piton or thread belay.

3 50 feet. Move to the right from the belay for 5 feet and climb the steep corner until a ledge on the left can be gained. Traverse left along the ledge, and then up the corner on to the slab of Great Eastern Route (pitch 5). Go up the step on to the higher slab. Indifferent rock belay or piton.

4 60 feet. Move about 15 feet along the slab to the right and climb the obvious groove to gain a ledge some 10 feet higher. Follow this back left into the corner below a poised pinnacle. Climb the green corner to a large slab stance. Piton or indifferent rock belay.

5 30 feet. Climb steeply up to the pinnacle on good holds. (The finishing holds need care). Avoid the pinnacle, which is delicately perched, and traverse to a ledge and chockstone belay.

6 70 feet. Step up to the left; then immediately move back diagonally to the right, up a steep little wall, to a ledge with more poised pinnacles. Climb the magnificent layback-crack at the back of the ledge to the top.

Great Eastern Route. 240 feet. Very severe (mild).

A fine climb with magnificent situations yet without great technical difficulty. A good introduction to the crag. The climb starts at an opening 15 feet to the right of the lowest part of the crag.

1 15 feet. Easy rocks are followed by a walk to the left. Stance and belay.

2 40 feet. Ascend without difficulty the cracked slab, which slants up to the left. After about 20 feet, an overhang is passed with difficulty, a layback move enabling a good hold on the right wall to be reached. Poor stance but good belay.

3 30 feet. Traverse left across the slab and climb the crack in the corner. Step round on to the face to the left, then straight up to a good stance and belay. (Yellow Slab Variation starts from here).

4 30 feet. The steep cracks ahead lead to a stance and belay. A roof juts out overhead.

5 35 feet. Cross the slab to the right and go up the step. There is a large, but inconspicuous flake belay about 15 feet to the right in a shallow corner (or use a piton on the slab).

6 40 feet. Ascend a little on good holds and continue the upward traverse to the right to a small crevasse.

7 30 feet. 10 feet higher is a shelf at the foot of a corner. It may be left by an easy chimney on the right, or by the left wall. Good belay.

8 20 feet. Climb up and round the corner on the right on good holds to a ledge at the top of the White Slab. Belay in the far corner.

Variation Start. 50 feet. Very severe (mild).
As hard as the original start, it avoids the overhang on pitch 2. Starts from the middle of the easy walk of pitch 1.

1a Ascend broken rocks and a short slab on the left to a large grassy ledge. Belay and poor stance a little higher on the left wall.

2a Continue up steep rock to the left to a large flat rock platform. Descend the extreme left corner for about 3 feet and traverse to the crack of pitch 2 above the overhang and just below the belay.

Variation Finish. **The Yellow Slab.** 175 feet. Very severe (hard).
This variation finish starts from a good belay and stance just above and to the left of the stance at the top of pitch 3. It is considerably harder than any part of the original route, giving superb climbing which, on the last pitch, becomes both delicate and exposed.

4a 30 feet. The crack on the left may be started direct or by pulling up on a small hold reached by standing on the point of the belay, then traversing in. The belay, suitable for line only, is close to the top of the crack. The stance is awkward and the leader may prefer to carry on to the top of the next pitch.

5a 80 feet. Climb the Yellow Slab until it finishes in a wall. Traverse left and discover a steep crack just around the corner. The crack lends itself to layback or jamming methods, and is strenuous. Break out left at the top to belay on a shelf.

6a 65 feet. Escape round the corner on the left, first climbing upwards with the help of a good flake, then working diagonally to the left. This pitch is exposed.

The climbs to the left of Great Eastern Route start from a terrace above a broken mass of rock and vegetation. From the foot of Great Eastern Route, the terrace is reached by a grass rake running up to the left for 30 feet.

Gold Rush. 400 feet. Extremely severe.

The route follows the hanging corner-crack, which gives excellent climbing, to the left of Yellow Slab. The start is a long way to the right, and is guarded by a wet corner, up the terrace about 40 feet left of Great Eastern.

1 130 feet. Pull over the steep walls on the right; then traverse left to the corner. Climb through the water to the overhang. Pull over this on improving holds to join Great Eastern (pitch 3) at the slab; continue up this climb to the good stance and belay at the top of pitch 3.

2 50 feet. Follow easy ledges horizontally left; then climb the black wall, and cross a short slab to a poor stance and piton belay below a long corner.

3 50 feet. Climb the excellent corner and crack direct to join The Yellow Slab Variation half-way up pitch 5a. Continue up the crack. Stance and chockstone belay at the top of pitch 5a of The Yellow Slab.

4 100 feet. Continue up the crack to the big overhang. Move out left with difficulty; then continue up the wall and slab above to a large ledge and piton belay.

5 70 feet. Easy climbing leads to the top.

The Overhanging Grooves. 290 feet. Extremely severe.

The route climbs direct the overhanging wall to the left of Great Eastern, which it crosses. It then follows a groove above The Yellow Slab to join The Centaur near the top of the crag. Although the first pitch requires considerable artificial aid, the upper pitches give excellent free climbing. The route starts from the terrace, below an obvious overhanging flake, 30 feet left of Gold Rush.

1 100 feet. Traverse to the right, up the wall, to reach the overhanging flake protecting the base of the first of three grooves coming down from Great Eastern. Climb over the flake to reach a natural chockstone runner. Traverse to the right across the impending wall (3 points of aid) to reach a niche in the central groove (runner). Move to the right on to a steep wall and, with aid from a nut, pull up into a little groove on Great Eastern. Continue to the stance and belay at the start of The Yellow Slab variation.

2 120 feet. Ascend the first pitch of The Yellow Slab. Continue up the crack above and then traverse to the right into a big groove above the roof seen from pitch 4 of Great Eastern. Ascend the groove (awkward to start and at half height) to the large stance and pinnacle on Centaur (top of pitch 5).

3 70 feet. Climb pitch 6 of The Centaur.

Ichabod. 240 feet. Extremely severe.

A fine climb of sustained difficulty and interest. The large overhanging wall on the left of the Overhanging Grooves ends at a prow of rock, which juts out, forming on its right a line of grooves and corners. The route follows this line. Below the prow are three parallel grooves or gangways slanting left. The climb starts in the right-hand one.

1 50 feet. Climb the easy gangway to a stance and belay below an impending crack leading to an overhung niche.

2 80 feet. Climb the crack, and from the niche make a delicate traverse to the right to reach a shallow corner. Climb the corner for 15 feet (piton), and step out to the right. The foot of a V-chimney is the next objective and it is reached either directly, or by a detour diagonally right followed by a horizontal traverse to the left. Excellent thread belay and stance in the chimney.

3 60 feet. Climb up the chimney and make an awkward exit left into a corner. Continue upwards on good holds to a ledge and belay below a steep crack.

4 50 feet. Climb the crack to a ledge and block belay.

Phoenix. 230 feet. Extremely severe.
An exposed and strenuous route of awe-inspiring steepness. The difficulties are well protected. The climb follows a groove up the overhanging prow of rock to the left of Ichabod, with which it shares the first pitch.

1 50 feet. The easy gangway is climbed to a stance and belay below an impending crack leading to an overhung niche.

2 90 feet. Either climb to the overhung niche and, with tension from a running belay on a flake, swing round the rib on the left into a groove, or enter the groove direct from the belay by a jamming crack. Both are equally difficult. Climb the overhanging crack above with difficulty (chockstone running belays), and make a strenuous pull-out to the left to a poor resting place in an airy situation. Protected by a piton, continue up the groove above and make another very difficult pull-out at the top, when the corner on the left can be

gained and climbed to a grass stance on the gangway above.

3 40 feet. Continue up the gangway to a good stance and pedestal belay.

4 50 feet. Climb straight up the corner above to the top.

Variation. Direct Finish. 140 feet. Very severe (hard).

3a 70 feet. From the belay above pitch 2 descend 5 feet and climb the wall above to good holds. Continue up for 20 feet; then traverse rightwards to the arête. Climb this to a large ledge and belay.

4a 70 feet. Climb up the easier ridge above.

Morning Wall. 210 feet. Very severe (mild).

This climb follows a diagonal line left from the foot of Ichabod, choosing the line of least resistance. The start is as for Ichabod.

1 40 feet. Climb the right-hand groove until a convenient opening allows a descent into the second groove to a good stance and large block belay.

2 25 feet. A vertical crack with a niche at its foot, and ill-supplied with holds, leads to a V-corner. Step over a rib to the left to a good stance and belay. (If necessary, the leader may climb this pitch with the aid of a shoulder).

3 25 feet. Continue the traverse along a widening ledge to a spike at the foot of a chimney.

4 50 feet. A step up to the left, and another back to the right lead into the chimney, which is climbed facing left. A little boulder pitch follows and leads to a large recess. There is a small belay high up on the right wall.

5 25 feet. The sloping slab on the left, with a wide easy crack in it, leads to a crevasse. Belays.

6 45 feet. Proceed up a recess to the left; then traverse along another crevassed block to the right to an easy chimney. Ascend this and finish up a cave pitch straight ahead.

Pegasus. 300 feet. Very severe (hard).

An exposed and delicate climb following a line below Morning Wall. The route starts at the same point as Morning Wall.

1 40 feet. Follow the leftward-slanting gangway to a stance and belay beneath the sentry box of Morning Wall.

2 85 feet. Traverse round the corner on the left, with the hands on a good flat ledge, and continue into a very steep open gully, just above the point where it merges into the large overhang, which extends to the bottom of the crag. (Running belay). A 6-foot chimney gives access to a steep gangway running up to the left. This is followed until it ends in a vertical corner, which forms the right-hand boundary of a grassy groove. To enter this groove, a rope through a piton may be used to help maintain balance. The groove is ascended for a few feet to a poor stance with belays.

3 45 feet. The grassy corner above is ascended until a steep V-groove is reached. This is ascended with difficulty (running belays) to a good ledge and belay below an overhang.

4 25 feet. The overhang forms a cave on the right. This is ascended and left by means of good holds in a crack on the right wall. Stance and belay near Morning Wall.

5 35 feet. Traverse the steep wall on the left on magnificent holds to an open chimney: stance and belay a few feet higher, below a crack.

6 25 feet. The crack is climbed, on good holds, to the left end of the amphitheatre below the last pitch of Morning Wall.

7 45 feet. Pitch 6 of Morning Wall.

Chimera. 255 feet. Very severe (hard).
A difficult and artificial first pitch, which can be avoided, is followed by pleasant free climbing up the grooves and walls above. Start 40 feet left of Morning Wall at an obvious break.

1 50 feet. The groove above the overhanging wall is gained with the aid of three pitons (blades, difficult to place) and two slings. From the groove move out right, and up on good holds to belay in a corner of Pegasus. (This belay is at the foot of the 6-foot chimney on pitch 2 of Pegasus, which can be climbed as an alternative to pitch 1 thereby making a completely free route).

2 55 feet. Gain the gangway on the left, and follow it to the piton on Pegasus (pitch 2). Climb the groove directly above the piton to a stance.

3 50 feet. Climb the corner above the stance and follow the continuation crack, steeply, to a large ledge and chockstone belay, (junction with Morning Wall).

4 100 feet. The fine crack in the wall above is followed to the top.

Hell's Groove. 265 feet. Very severe (hard).
A serious climb of absorbing technical interest, following an obvious deep groove protected by a short overhanging wall, and joining Pegasus in its upper pitches. To reach the start traverse some 80 feet to the left of Ichabod, descending 10 feet at one point where the terrace changes level.

1 30 feet. Climb an easy slab to a stance and belay below the overhanging crack.

2 25 feet. The crack appears to be straighforward, but overhangs in two directions and is very strenuous. Above the crack enter the main groove. Belays but poor stance.

3 80 feet. A magnificent pitch. Climb on to a sloping ledge in the corner of the groove. Pull out to the right into a crack and ascend to a 2-foot wide sloping ledge. Continue straight up to another ledge with a small block at the right-hand end for a running belay. A vertical 10-foot wall above gives access to a crack, which provides good holds for the ascent to the ledge above pitch 3 of Pegasus. The final move on to the ledge is awkward.

4 25 feet.
5 35 feet.
6 25 feet.
7 45 feet.
} As for the corresponding pitches of Pegasus

Variation. Direct Finish. 120 feet. Very severe (hard).

5a 40 feet. Move up to the right into the large recess of Morning Wall. Belay below a steep green crack.

6a 60 feet. Climb the green, overhanging crack directly above the belay, and continue to a small cave (belay).

7a 20 feet. Go straight up over the block, which forms the roof, to the top of the crag.

Incubus†. 200 feet. Extremely severe.
A steep and technically interesting climb, taking a bold line between Hell's Groove and Trinity. Starts at the same point as Trinity.

1 70 feet. Climb up to gain a small ledge; then work up to the right, until a short traverse to the right beneath an overhang can be made. Reach up a thin crack, place a piton and use it to get on to the wall above; then place another, pull up from this, and climb up to the

† This route has not been checked by the guide writers.

right to gain a final piton (in place). Continue straight up, with increasing difficulty, until a step to the right leads to sloping stance, (piton belay).

2 70 feet. Climb the crack near the edge, directly above the stance; at its top, move left and up to gain the "inserted nut runner", (junction with Holy Ghost, which is followed to the stance).

3 60 feet. Move up left above the stance; then traverse a short distance left round the corner. Pull up and step right on to a slab. Continue a little further right until below a shallow groove; finish up this.

Trinity. 225 feet. Very severe (hard).

A good route following a natural line up the crag. The difficulties are well protected. The climb starts below the obvious steep groove 20 feet left of Hell's Groove.

1 20 feet. Climb up to a stance and belay at the foot of the long groove.

2 80 feet. Move straight up the groove to the overhang. Climb this on its left to a large ledge. Stance and belay.

3 95 feet. Continue over the bulge in the corner on to a slab. Go straight up the slab to the overhanging corner crack, layback up the crack, and step on to a slab on the left. Move diagonally leftwards to the foot of a short wall (junction with Gremlin's Groove), and climb this to a large grass ledge. Perched block belay on the front of the ledge or an inserted chockstone belay in a crack. Alternatively, from the top of the layback crack, continue directly upwards on steep rock, which soon eases, and the same stance and belay is reached.

4 30 feet. Climb the corner and crack above to the top.

Holy Ghost. 270 feet. Extremely severe.

A technically exacting and exposed climb, which follows a somewhat contrived line diagonally right from Gremlin's Groove, crossing over Trinity before reaching the top of the crag. The climb starts at the same point as Gremlin's Groove.

1 100 feet. Climb Gremlin's Groove for 40 feet until it is possible to traverse to the right across a series of sloping ledges. A pull up a steep wall leads to the left end of a ledge at the top of pitch 2 of Trinity.

2 50 feet. Climb the corner behind the belay for 10 feet; then move right and slightly downwards on a line of holds leading round the corner to a small roof on the nose. Using undercut handholds, move under this and pull up to the right, continuing the traverse on rounded holds for a further 10 feet, until it is possible to climb straight up a steep slab. (The traverse can be continued a few feet to take advantage of an inserted nut running belay, in place). Climb the slab and trend left, (piton belay in a shallow scoop).

3 50 feet. Traverse to the right and climb up a groove to a ledge.

4 70 feet. Climb the steep crack to the top of a huge flake and, from its top, pull straight up the overhanging crack and so to the top of the crag.

There is a series of three cracks or grooves near the left-hand end of the buttress. The right-hand one is Gremlin's Groove, and the second (8 feet to the left) the variation start. The final crack is the line of Slime Chimney, which is reached by climbing a 6-foot wall and going under a cave.

The Gremlin's Groove. 175 feet. Very severe.

A pleasant climb, lacking the seriousness of its neighbours on the right. The route starts up the right one of two cracks or grooves breaking the crag some 30 feet left of Trinity.

1 80 feet. The groove is followed to its end. (Jammed flakes and chockstone may be used for running belays). This pitch is steeper than it appears from below. Stance and belay by perched blocks.

2 25 feet. Bear right to a good rock ledge and flake belay.

3 45 feet. Climb up to the overhang; then step to the right to a good rock ledge. (Line running belay). Climb the short vertical wall to a big grassy ledge with a block belay at its right-hand end.

4 25 feet. Awkward ledges are climbed to the foot of a layback-crack which is followed to the top.

Variation Start. Goes up the steep crack 8 feet to the left of Gremlin's Groove.

1a 30 feet. Climb the steep wall on the left of the crack until entry can be made into the crack. The crack is then climbed to a stance and large belay.

2a 20 feet. Climb the wall on the right of the crack for a few feet; then move to the right on to the rib; go up this for a few feet, then traverse to the right into Gremlin's Groove at the level of the first overhang and continue up the normal route.

Slime Chimney. 90 feet. Very difficult.

1 20 feet. Climb the slanting rock steps to a ledge and belay.

2 40 feet. Go up the vertical crack in the corner.

3 15 feet. Gully climbing; this section is green and often wet.

4 15 feet. An easy chimney is climbed to the top.

South Chimney. 205 feet. Very severe (hard).

This route starts at a crevassed block on a grass terrace about 60 feet lower than and to the left of the start of Slime Chimney and Gremlin's Groove. It finishes up the wide, open chimney seen on the skyline of the southern corner of the crag, the chimney running up to the right of an obvious overhanging nose. A rather dirty, lichenous route whose justification lies in the long final pitch which gives pleasant climbing.

1 65 feet. Follow the open chimney past the overhanging section, which is capped with turf (at present), to a grass ledge and block belay. (At 25 feet a poor stance and good thread belay can be taken, but it is better for the leader to continue straight through).

2 35 feet. Follow easy broken rocks and then a little slab to a good grass ledge with a belay at its left end.

3 15 feet. Climb rock ledges, bearing left to a good ledge and belay.

4 90 feet. Take the line of least resistance up the chimney.

There are two girdle traverses of the East Buttress. The original route, which does not traverse the whole of the crag (right to left) is considerably easier than the more recent route, which traverses the whole crag from left to right.

East Buttress Girdle. About 750 feet. Very severe (hard). A first-class expedition, the severity being quite well sustained. Starts from Mickledore Chimney and traverses the face of the crag to finish up the Yellow Slab.

1 70 feet. Pitch 1 of Mickledore Grooves, Slab Start.

2 40 feet. Pitch 2 of Mickledore Grooves, Slab Start. After traversing the slab, the leader can leave a line sling on a small spike above and to the left of the ledge to safeguard the second man. Descend a few feet to a ledge and block belays at the top of pitch 2 of Mickledore Grooves.

3 10 feet. Climb the corner above the stance to a good flake belay and small stance.

4 20 feet. A delicate horizontal traverse to the left is followed by an awkward step round the corner into a groove. Stance and moderate belay.

5 50 feet. First make a descending traverse to the left and cross the next groove; then climb from the end of a sloping ledge into a corner (this is awkward to start but it becomes easier once an entry has been gained). 20 feet higher there is a large grassy ledge with belays.

6 15 feet. Ascend the corner at the extreme left of the ledge to a stance and belay.

7 80 feet. Cross the top of the large slab and descend it towards its left end (pitch 6 of May Day). Small spike belay.

8 20 feet. Descend an easy scoop (pitch 5 of May Day), to the belay at the top of a crack.

9 15 feet. Traverse left to Overhanging Wall and descend to a grass ledge and belay overlooking the White Slab.

10 25 feet. From the belay descend 5 feet; then traverse delicately over a nose for 20 feet. Small belay in corner.

11 60 feet. Descend to the White Slab; then climb it to a position just below the large square block in its centre. Belay round the block. (White Slab Variation, pitch 2).

12 70 feet. Traverse easily left, then along a platform to a corner. Traverse to the left out of the corner for a few feet and ascend the wall for 25 feet to the crevasse at the top of pitch 6 of Great Eastern Route. Belay.

13 40 feet. Descend pitch 6 Great Eastern Route to the flake belay (or piton belay on the slab).

14 35 feet. Descend Pitch 5 of Great Eastern Route.

15 30 feet. Descend Pitch 4 of Great Eastern Route to belay at the junction with the Yellow Slab Variation.

16 30 feet.
17 80 feet.
18 60 feet.
} Follow pitches 4, 5 and 6 of the Yellow Slab variation.

The Lord of the Rings†. 1,210 feet. Extremely severe.
A magnificent climb, taking an eliminate line across the crag from left to right. All members of the team should be competent on this serious route.

1 100 feet. Pitch 1 of Holy Ghost.

2 80 feet. Continue pitch 2 of Holy Ghost as far as the nut runner. Descend the wall below, first to the right, then move left and down to the right, to a ledge overlooking Hell's Groove, (piton belay on the arête).

3 50 feet. Move round into the groove; then traverse to the right to join Hell's Groove, which is climbed to the stance (top of pitch 2).

4 100 feet. Move to the right over a grass ledge; then go down a groove for a few feet until moves to the right to Morning Wall can be made. Descend the gangway to the base of a pinnacle/flake and climb its left side to the top. Using tension from a nut, traverse the narrow ledge to the rib, pull up and climb across to the stance on Phoenix (pitch 2).

5 50 feet. Follow the Direct Finish to Phoenix, as far as the arête, (belay).

6 60 feet. Descend the steep wall for about 25 feet; then move to the right, into Ichabod above the awkward exit from the chimney on pitch 3. Step down and hand-traverse to the right; then pull up, and continue to a ledge, (piton belay).

7 60 feet. Cross the slab, and descend the bottomless groove for 6 feet to a small ledge. Move round the arête to join The Yellow Slab; descend this to the awkward stance at the top of pitch 4a, (piton belay).

8 30 feet. Descend pitch 4a of The Yellow Slab to the good stance and belay on Great Eastern Route (pitch 3).

† This route has not been checked by the guide writers.

9 80 feet. Follow a descending ledge line on the right, until the obvious line of holds on Centaur are reached; follow these to the stance top of pitch 2 of Centaur, (piton or thread belay).

10 80 feet. Follow Centaur for 15 feet; then go straight up the steep wall, (piton runner down to the right), and pull up on to a small sloping ledge with difficulty, (piton runner above to safeguard the second). Traverse right, gradually descending; then move up and across to a small, yellow, sloping ledge on top of a prominent prow, (piton belay).

11 20 feet. Climb the groove above to a large ledge on Armagedon (pitch 6). Piton belay.

12 50 feet. Follow the line of large ledges to the right, round the corner to the large black belay, (top of pitch 5a of The White Slab).

13 50 feet. Descend to the foot of The White Slab.

14 100 feet. Round the rib on the right, move down and step to the right. Climb up and follow a descending line to a rib; round this to the friction stance, (top of pitch 2 of May Day Climb).

15 80 feet. Pitch 3a of May Day Direct Finish.

16 50 feet. Reverse pitch 5 of the East Buttress Girdle.

17 30 feet. Reverse pitches 4 and 3 of the East Buttress Girdle.

18 140 feet. Pitch 3 of Mickledore Grooves.

CAM SPOUT CRAG (216057)

This is the crag to the south-west of Cam Spout clearly seen on the left of the beck when approaching from Eskdale. (For the approach routes see Esk Buttress).

Apart from a couple of forays early in the century the crag escaped serious notice until the 1960's, when explorers discovered that the scale of the cliff was much larger than it appeared from the track below.

The main features of the crag are the deeply-cut Peregrine Gully and the steep grooved buttress on its left. Most of the climbs are located in this area. The rest of the crag is broken and covered with vegetation.

The best means of descent is by a large rake slanting down from right to left (true right), which is reached by scrambling some two hundred feet above the finish of the climbs.

The climbs are described from right to left.

The Spout. 200 feet. Very severe.

Scramble up Peregrine Gully for several hundred feet until the gully widens out. On the right wall of the gully (true left) is a series of grooves, which appears from below to be deceptively easy-angled. Start from a bilberry ledge a few feet above the bed of the gully.

1 40 feet. The slanting groove-gangway is climbed to a stance beneath the hanging crack.

2 40 feet. Climb the hanging crack direct and make an exit left, by a detached flake, to a good ledge and belays.

3 80 feet. Climb the chimney behind the belay, taking care with loose blocks, and swing into the bottom of the steep groove. Step left, out of the groove, and round on to the slab; climb this direct to a large flake. Attain the top of the flake, and step delicately to the right, into the groove again, and climb it to good ledges and belay.

4 40 feet. Easy scrambling leads to broken ground and the top of the crag.

Peregrine Gully

It contains a mixture of loose scree, boulders, earth and a little climbing on rotten rock near the top.

Vargtime. 190 feet. Very severe (hard).

An interesting climb which ascends the big groove-fault in the overhanging right wall of Cam Spout Buttress (the true right wall of Peregrine Gully). Start from a grass ledge level with the first chockstone in the gully, where a low overhanging wall bars access to the groove.

1 90 feet. Pull over the short overhanging wall with difficulty. Climb the groove, passing wedged blocks, to a recess capped by an overhang. Move out to the right, on to the rib, and ascend to a large grass ledge and good belays.

2 100 feet. Climb the steep corner at the back of the bay, on excellent finger jams, for about 20 feet. Move right and up, strenuously, to a slab blocked by an overhang. Traverse to the right, across the slab, until the overhang is outflanked; then climb up, awkwardly, to gain a ledge overlooking the gully. Continue up easier broken rock to grass ledges and a belay.

Cam Spout Buttress. 260 feet. Very severe (hard).

Follow the right end of the buttress, starting just left of the foot of Peregrine Gully, where an easy-looking ridge leads up to a short steep red wall.

1 45 feet. The ridge is climbed to a ledge. Block belay at the left-hand end.

2 60 feet. From the block make a hard pull-up; then go left, up a rake, to a grass ledge below a wall with two thin cracks. Climb these to the foot of a thin overhanging crack. Traverse left to a belay at the foot of another overhanging crack.

3 40 feet. Climb the overhanging crack (care with a doubtful block). Step left at the top and go up to a juniper belay at the back of the ledge below a smooth slab.

4 55 feet. Climb the slab up its left-hand side.

5 60 feet. Pull over the overhang about 8 feet right of the overhanging crack; then step back left into the crack, which is climbed to the top.
150 feet of easy scrambling leads to the slanting rake.

Manhanger. 230 feet. Very severe (hard).

The route climbs the right edge of the upper wall, a short distance to the right of Eskdale Grooves. Start as for Cam Spout Buttress.

1 70 feet. Follow Cam Spout buttress for 40 feet to the large detached blocks below a short, steep wall. Traverse horizontally left, with difficulty round a bulge; then go up left to attain a triangular grass ledge and good belays below an indistinct groove in the left edge of the buttress.

2 100 feet. Climb the groove above the stance, first on the right using cracks, then cross the groove at its top, and follow grass ledges leftwards. Go up an easy-angled groove to belay in a small corner, just to the right of the final steep groove.

3 60 feet. Follow an easy ramp leftwards to reach the final groove. Climb this, with increasing difficulty, until an overhang near the top prevents further progress. At this point the groove divides. Move out of the main groove into the right-hand branch, with difficulty, and follow this to the top.

Eskdale Grooves. 230 feet. Very severe (hard).

The route starts as for Cam Spout Grooves and climbs the big corner to its right. The final groove is very strenuous. Start directly below the corner, at the first small clump of junipers, 20 yards to the left of Peregrine Gully.

1 100 feet. Climb directly up the broken wall, making a move left over an overlap and into a groove at 40 feet. Continue up the groove to a large grassy stance with good belays below a cave at the foot of the corner.

2 80 feet. Climb up to the roof, and step to the right, across a slab, into the corner. Climb the big corner direct to a grass ledge and good belays below the final steep groove.

3 50 feet. Climb the groove to an overlap, using a nut and spike for aid. Make a difficult move on to the slab above; then swing left, round a rib, and up grass ledges to belays.

Cam Spout Grooves. 295 feet. Very severe.

A route of character. Takes a line of square-cut grooves just to the right of the very prominent overhanging rib, which starts about 100 feet above a grassy gully. Starts as for Eskdale Grooves.

1 40 feet. Easy-angled rocks lead up left, with a long stride at one point, to a stance below a short steep wall, which runs up to the right. Belay 10 feet higher.

2 80 feet. Follow the crack against the overlap for 15 feet to a heathery ledge. Climb the overlapping wall, steeply, on good holds and step left on to grassy slabs above the overlap. Continue easily, to a large sloping triangular ledge below an overhang. Belay.

3 35 feet. Make an awkward movement up and round to the left; then climb up to the big ledge below the steep corner.

4 60 feet. Climb the corner-crack to the top of a large flake on the left at 20 feet. Move back into the corner and up to another large triangular ledge. Spike belay in the corner.

5 75 feet. From the lower left-hand end of the ledge, step round into the big corner on the left. This is climbed first to a small ledge (runner) on the left, and then on the left wall and rib, turning the overhang at the top by a move left round the corner. A short delicate wall, in an airy situation, completes the climb.

The Ent. 385 feet. Very severe.

Takes a line up the big corner on the left of the prominent overhanging rib which lies to the left of Cam Spout Grooves. Starts at the bottom of the grassy gully directly below the rib.

1 100 feet. Climb the gully for 10 feet; then move to the right round a bulge and up to a grassy ledge. Move up to a small clump of junipers below an overlap; then traverse left and climb up to the bottom of an open mossy groove. Move back right into a clean-cut V-groove and climb this to a grass ledge and spike belay. There is much vegetation on this pitch at present.

2 130 feet. An excellent pitch. Move left and ascend the groove to a small ledge below the big corner. Surmount the bulge, (piton in place), and climb the corner to a small ledge. Traverse the slab on the left to the very exposed rib. Climb the rib to a small stance at the bottom of an open groove. Belay on a flat-topped spike on the right.

3 80 feet. Climb straight up the groove; then move left and up a short white slab to a groove on the right. Ascend this to a large stance and thread belay, low down.

4 25 feet. Move through the crevasse on the right.

5 50 feet. Climb up the right-hand edge of the slabs above, overlooking Peregrine Gully.

100 feet of scrambling leads to the top.

The Orc. 350 feet. Very severe (hard).

A direct route, following The Ent in places and taking in the difficulties which that route by-passes. Start as for the Ent.

1 90 feet. Climb the grassy gully for 20 feet; then move up the right wall to a grass ledge. Move up to a small clump of junipers, then left into an open mossy groove, (the Ent goes right at this point). Climb the groove to a grass ledge and belay.

2 130 feet. As for The Ent to the small ledge above the piton. Continue up the corner with difficulty, mainly by finger jamming, to a large flake. Continue, more easily, to a huge block belay, but no stance.

3 80 feet. Surmount the bulge above the belays and climb up the groove, moving to the right below an overhang to a grass ledge. Alternatively, surmount the bulge and traverse to the right on to the exposed rib, which is ascended to the grass ledge.

4 50 feet. Climb up the slabs above to the finish.

Blarney†. 500 feet. Very severe (hard).

A somewhat broken route, but with some interesting and exposed climbing. About 50 yards left of The Ent, and 150 feet up the crag is an overhanging buttress with a pale green streak in the centre. Start below this at a large block.

1 60 feet. Climb up directly behind the block to a grass ledge.

2 60 feet. Move right for 10 feet; then go up the wall above, trending right to a cleaned, slanting, V-groove. Climb this, and move out to the right to a small stance.

3 80 feet. Hand-traverse to the right into the overhanging chimney. Climb this, moving out right with difficulty on to grass; then go up to large blocks below an overhang.

4 80 feet. Go up the grassy ramp on the left for 30 feet;

† This route has not been checked by the guide writers.

then move to the right on to the exposed slab. Cross this, delicately, and move up to a small stance below a small juniper with an overhanging corner above.

5 40 feet. Traverse left and go up the steep wall above, with difficulty, (sling for aid), to a grass ledge. Spike belay up on the left.

6 30 feet. Ascend the short overhanging chimney above.

7 50 feet. Scramble up steep grass to a belay.

8 100 feet. A jamming crack on the right leads to the exposed rib, which is followed, pleasantly, to the top.

Existentialism. 200 feet. Very severe.
This poor route, only its first pitch being of any merit, climbs the buttress to the left of Blarney. Start 30 feet left and 100 feet above the large spike, which marks the start of Blarney.

1 80 feet. Climb the groove in the front of the nose, on awkwardly-sloping holds, to the foot of a flake-crack. The flake appears sound and is climbed to a belay on a grassy ramp below a short corner.

2 80 feet. Climb the corner, moving out left on good holds. Continue up to good stance and belays.

3 40 feet. Move left and up the rib on suspect rock. Scramble easily to the top.

SCAFELL PIKE

PIKE'S CRAG

The crag is on the west side of Scafell Pike and is to the north of Mickledore, in full view from Hollow Stones. It is more broken than Scafell Crag and, comparatively, the routes are lacking in both character and seriousness. However, its south-facing aspect can give warm, dry climbing on indifferent days. The climbs are described from right to left, i.e. in order from the south (Mickledore) to north (Lingmell).

Mickledore Buttress No. 1. 100 feet. Difficult.
The climb goes up the buttress nearest to Mickledore and starts at the foot of a chimney, almost in the middle of the face.

1 20 feet. A wall is climbed to a ledge and belay.

2 20 feet. Climb the chimney; the finish over the large boulder may be taken on either side. Stance and belay on top of the boulder.

3 20 feet. The little wall on the left has good holds and leads to a comfortable platform. Belay.

4 40 feet. A series of cracks, with good holds, trend left. Belay.

Mickledore Buttress, Western Corner. 120 feet. Difficult.
This is the fairly well-defined buttress rising on the right of a deep scree gully, which cuts off the Pulpit Rock on the south. After a little scrambling a ledge is reached below a definite wall.

1 30 feet. A groove, slanting to the left, is climbed to a niche. Belay.

2 35 feet. The left-hand one of two steep cracks is taken to a stance and belay.

3 35 feet. The route goes round the corner on the right, then straight up, working leftwards to a ledge and belay.

4 20 feet. The easy scrambling may be avoided by climbing the projecting nose of the buttress. Cairn. An almost vertical wall cuts off the buttress from the fell. The neck may be reached by an abseil, or the ridge running down to the right may be descended. There is a very awkward movement down a short wall about 20 feet from the top; the rest is fairly easy.

Pulpit Rock

This is the high mass of rock in the centre of Pike's Crag. It is cut off from the fell by deep gullies, branches of which run up from both sides and join at a neck high up behind the summit. The wall so formed is most easily climbed by a 30-foot chimney, which starts a little to the south of the neck, and finishes near the highest point.

Cremation Ridge. 365 feet. Difficult.
The climb which starts from the right-hand gully at a point where it bends left, runs up a jagged ridge to the summit of Pulpit Rock. Short pitches of little interest.

Pulpit Rock is subtended by a stretch of broken rock, varying from 30 feet to 70 feet in height, crowned by a fairly well-marked grass terrace from which the next ten climbs start.

Southern Corner. 235 feet. Severe.
The climb starts below a slab, about 20 feet to the right and above the foot of a very clearly marked arête, which falls straight from the highest point of the crag.

1 70 feet. Climb the slab for about 30 feet, when diminishing holds force a move off to the right by a large block. Continue up grass and gain a stance on the right at some blocks. Small belay on the wall.

2 25 feet. Climb the left-hand corner for a few feet and, after an awkward movement to the right, finish up the arête on sloping holds. Belay.

3 45 feet. The corner of the ridge above is climbed and grass leads to a belay.

4 35 feet. Slant to the right, on grass and rock, to a cairn below a chimney with chockstones.

5 20 feet. The chimney may be climbed, or for cleaner rock, the wall on the left. Easy rocks follow. Belay.

6 40 feet. The steep ridge ahead has good holds and leads to several large blocks.

A short distance above the end of Southern Corner there is an easy descent into the scree gully running up behind Pulpit Rock. It is also possible to reach the top of the Rock by scrambling up either grass ledges on the right, or easy rocks on the left, to a huge boulder with a cairn on it where the last pitch of the Grooved Arête may be followed to the summit.

Sector. 405 feet. Severe (mild).

A semi-circular excursion of Pulpit Rock, which starts up Southern Corner, traverses the crag and finishes at the top of Wall and Crack; the descent of the latter almost completes the circle.

1 70 feet.
2 25 feet. } Climb pitches 1, 2 and 3 of Southern Corner.
3 45 feet.

4 20 feet. Climb the slab on the left to a good belay and small stance in a crack behind a large detached flake.

5 20 feet. Descend a step or two and continue horizontally to a grassy stance. Belay.

6 60 feet. Descend a few feet to a large jammed boulder and move over the slightly impending left wall of the corner. The crack slanting diagonally up to the main rib on the left is now the objective and this leads on to Grooved Arête. Stance and belay.

7 50 feet. Walk up into a recess and follow the grass ledge to the left. Climb over a projecting boulder and reach a good stance and belay before a short wall.

8 15 feet. Cross the rather smooth wall to another good ledge and belay.

9 35 feet. Descend into a dirty corner where a convenient line of holds allows smooth slabs to be crossed; then grass leads into a corner with a moderate belay.

10 25 feet. Step down a little and then climb over the low wall on the left to a large sloping grass ledge, which is followed to a collection of blocks below a steep crack.

11 25 feet. Climb the crack to a recess below the final pitch of Juniper Buttress. A few feet to the left is an upstanding bollard of rock, which gives an excellent belay.

12 15 feet. A delicate crossing of the steep wall on the left is made on to the Wall and Crack Climb.

Slanting Groove. 340 feet. Severe (hard).

The climb, which starts as for Grooved Arête, follows the corner-groove on the right side of that route.

1 60 feet. As for Grooved Arête, to a belay below the steep crack.

2 70 feet. Climb the right-hand sloping crack to a large spike below the overhang. Turn this by a slab on the right, and move up to a grass ledge and belay.

3 40 feet. Move up to the right, to a small overhang; then go back left into a leaning crack, which leads to a belay in the corner.

4 70 feet. Climb the left wall, and move back immediately into the groove, which is ascended to a choice of stances and belays.

5 70 feet. Continue up the groove to a belay below a large overhanging block.

6 30 feet. Move left to join Grooved Arête, at the small chimney on the left of the block. Follow Grooved Arête to the top.

Grooved Arête. 370 feet. Very difficult.

A good climb, which starts below a noticeable hollow just on the right of the arête, which falls from the highest point of the crag.

1 60 feet. Move off to the right and enter an easy grassy groove running back to the left. This is followed to a stance and belay at the foot of a steep crack.

2 40 feet. The crack is climbed for 25 feet and a traverse is taken to the arête on the left, which is climbed to a grass ledge. Belay in the chimney a little distance back.

3 70 feet. The chimney is climbed and, about 25 feet up, the chimney is left with some difficulty for a steep grass continuation. (A large, poised boulder should be avoided). Grassy ledges follow and lead into a rectangular corner where there is a thread belay in the right-hand crack.

4 55 feet. The crack in the right-hand corner is hard to start. When a ledge is reached, traverse to the left a little then up to a pile of blocks. Continue up a few feet and make a pleasant traverse to the right to a prominent block on the edge of the ridge.

5 60 feet. Climb the slab ahead, work to the left, and then cross over to a series of ledges on the edge. Block belay.

6 25 feet. Step over the corner on the left and continue up a slab to a ledge below a huge block with a cairn on it. Belay.

7 15 feet. Climb the chimney on the left of the block. It is possible to leave the climb here and to descend into the scree gully just beyond.

8 45 feet. Walk along a ledge running down to the left on the wall above the gap and gain the front of the rock again. The slab which follows is difficult, and is climbed direct to the summit of the Pulpit Rock.

Variation. Slabs Direct—This is an alternative to pitches 3 and 4 of Grooved Arête and takes a more natural, if harder, line up the slabs than the original route. Severe.

3a 80 feet. Starting from the ledge above the crack of pitch 2, step on to the nose of the slab ahead and follow the edge to a platform (about 30 feet) beyond which there is a steep step in the slab. After surmounting this step by a delicate move, follow the slab, first to a small ledge and then on the right edge to a grass ledge. Belay a few feet left on the ordinary route.

4a 50 feet. Climb the slab above on good holds until a vertical crack is reached. Follow this, and, after passing a small bulge, bear right then left, and finally right again. In another 15 feet the prominent block at the top of pitch 4 of the ordinary route is reached.

Wriggling Route. 400 feet. Very severe.

A series of variations on Grooved Arête using throughout the belays of the latter and following, more or less (at will), the true line of the arête giving interesting climbing.

Urchin's Groove. 330 feet. Severe (hard).

The route follows a series of grooves taking the natural line of ascent up the dirty, mossy (and usually wet) hollow, which runs up the centre of Pulpit Rock. Not recommended.

1 45 feet. Climb the corner easily for about 20 feet, then take an awkward step up and to the right on to a grass ledge. Belay in the groove to the left of the ledge.

2 30 feet. Climb the groove on small holds. An awkward finish is made over grass to a good ledge. Belay around a chockstone in a crack on the left.

3 50 feet. Traverse to the right into the groove and climb to an overhang which is avoided by a delicate step left. Move back to the right; the finish over grass is awkward. Good flake belay.

4 40 feet. The groove behind the belay is followed to an overhang. Make a step to the right on to a rib which is then followed to a corner with a good flake belay.

5 55 feet. Ascend an easy groove straight ahead to a ledge on the left. Belay.

6 60 feet. Easy ledges on the left lead to a corner at the foot of a steep crack. Belay.

7 50 feet. Climb the crack on good holds. Easier climbing then leads out to ledges and the route finishes below a prominent poised block.

The Sentinel. 265 feet. Very severe.

The best of the harder routes on the crag giving very pleasant climbing. The route starts at the right-hand corner of the steep rib, which bounds on the left the green mossy gully of Urchin's Groove, and goes up the large square-cut pillar, which is the main feature of the centre of Pulpit Rock. It follows the obvious thin crack straight up the face of the pillar.

1 60 feet. Steep delicate climbing first up the rib, then trending left, leads to a grass ledge and belay.

2 80 feet. Climb straight up above the ledge for 15 feet to an overhang split by a crack. Climb the bulging crack to a good resting place on the left. Avoid some loose flakes by moving right and then back again into the crack, which is climbed direct up the smooth wall to the top of the pillar.

3 65 feet. Easier climbing leads up to a stance and belay below and to the left of an obvious overhanging crack (which can be seen on the skyline).

4 60 feet. Climb straight up to the overhang and over it, avoiding a doubtful block. Continue straight up the crack, pleasant climbing leading up to a stance and belay on easy ground.

The Citadel. 355 feet. Very severe.

The route starts about 15 feet left of the Sentinel at a shallow crack in the steep and continuous rib, which bounds Urchin's Groove on the left.

1 50 feet. Ascend the crack direct to a good grass ledge and belay.

2 15 feet. An easy crack on the right is climbed to another ledge and belay.

3 30 feet. Climb the steep slab on the right edge of the wall to a point where a short traverse leads to the right and round the corner to a roomy recess. Thread belay.

4 35 feet. Climb the steep crack to a small rock ledge. Thread belay. The next section of the crack is climbed on hand and foot jams. Good holds soon appear and a comfortable ledge is reached. Belay.

5 60 feet. Climb the delightful slabs above, following the line of least resistance to a recess with a large block belay.

6 45 feet. Make a short traverse to the right over rock and grass; then climb broken slabs to a recess with thread belay.

7 15 feet. An easy gully is followed to the ledge on the right. Large flake belay.

8 45 feet. From the flake step into the gully, then out on to the slab on the right. Grass stance and belay 12 feet right of the main corner.

9 60 feet. Climb a narrowing chimney on the right, until it is possible to step out to the right and follow a rib to easy ground and belay.

Juniper Buttress. 250 feet. Very difficult.

A good face climb, which starts at a large detached block to the left of the Citadel and about 50 yards to the right of the left bounding rib of Pulpit Rock.

1 35 feet. From the block a ledge is reached and a traverse made to the right into a corner below a crack (runner). The crack is climbed and left near the top in favour of the arête. Ledge and belay.

2 25 feet. Climb a furrow slanting up the wall to the right past a doubtful-looking arrow. Grass ledge and belay.

3 35 feet. Climb over a series of blocks to the left, finishing up a rather difficult crack. Belay.

4 50 feet. Ascend grass, and then rocks, working to the right to a stance and belay on the edge of a grassy gully.

5 55 feet. A groove above and to the left, followed by a crack lead to a shelf with a recess at its back. Belays.

6 50 feet. The exposed wall above is climbed by a thin crack, starting at a rib just to the right. A stretch of easy scrambling leads to the top of the Pulpit Rock.

Wall and Crack Climb. 270 feet. Very difficult.

An enjoyable climb, which follows, more or less, the left-hand ridge of Pulpit Rock.

1 35 feet. Step round on to the left of the ridge and climb to a stance and belay.

2 30 feet. A steep wall is climbed to a ledge and belay.

3 20 feet. A vertical crack, or the face to the right of it is climbed to a rock platform with large block belay.

4 30 feet. Starting on the right, a staircase of rock is ascended to a terrace (thread belays).

5 35 feet. The wall above is climbed from right to left on improving holds.

6 35 feet. Climb a crack running up to the right in three risers.

7 35 feet. A rock staircase leads to a ledge. A short distance above the ledge is a belay, on the right, at the foot of a crack.

8 50 feet. The almost vertical crack or the wall on its left, is followed by easier rocks. Scrambling follows to the top.

To the left of Wall and Crack and divided from it by a grassy gully is a small buttress, Mare's Nest Buttress which, when viewed from Hollow Stones seems to possess a sharp rock pinnacle (the Mare's Nest).

Mare's Nest Buttress. 125 feet. Very severe (mild).
The route runs up the right edge of the face of the buttress. From the foot of the gully, mount some grassy ledges to the foot of a grassy groove which is below a large overhang.

1 90 feet. Step on to the rib on the left of the groove and follow this until it runs into a grassy crack leading up to the overhang. Using the right wall, ascend until an obvious traverse line leads rightwards to a small ledge on the rib. Climb the rib bearing rightwards, to a large grass ledge with belays on the edge of 'D' gully.

2 35 feet. Climb easy rocks above the belay and bear left to join Pike's Crag Ridge, which is followed to the top.

Mare's Rib. 165 feet. Very severe.
After a short subsidiary rib, the route follows the obvious rib running up to the centre of the face between two sets of overhangs; it then follows the easiest line up the face. The climb starts at a large spike belay below and about 15 feet to the left of Mare's Nest Buttress.

1 120 feet. Climb up the rib straight above the belay for 20 feet; then step left on to the main rib, which leads to a steep crack on the face. Climb this for 10 feet then move diagonally to the right to a good stance. Belay.

2 45 feet. Climb straight up to the large overhanging block. Step left underneath this and climb the crack above. Easier climbing then leads to the top of the buttress and to Pike's Crag Ridge.

Osiris. 210 feet. Very severe.
Starts at the same point as Isis, at the foot of the arête forming the left edge of Mare's Nest Buttress.

1 40 feet. Climb the arête to a ledge and belay.

2 130 feet. Climb a short crack on the right; then traverse diagonally right, below the overhangs, to the foot of a short corner, which splits them. Climb the corner for 25 feet to a good flake. Traverse left into a leftward-slanting groove, which is climbed to a ledge and belay.

3 40 feet. The wide crack on the right, followed by easy rock, leads to the top.

Isis. 180 feet. Very severe (mild).

A pleasant little climb, which takes the left-hand arête of Mare's Nest Buttress. Start at the foot of the arête, as for Osiris.

1 40 feet. As for Osiris.

2 100 feet. Step left, and climb a steep crack in a scoop to the foot of an easy-angled corner-groove. Climb this, using the left arête as necessary, to a ledge with a large pedestal. Chock belay.

3 40 feet. From the pedestal, pull on to the wall above, move to the right, round the corner, and up a crack to join Pike's Crag Ridge. Finish up or down Pike's Crag Ridge.

Pike's Crag Ridge. 430 feet. Very difficult.

The climb starts at the foot of 'D' Gully and goes up the buttress to the right. On the 5th pitch, the buttress ends and the broken ridge can be followed to the final summit wall. Alternatively a descent can be made to the foot of the crag via the gully on the right. The actual climbing starts after scrambling up grassy ledges to the foot of a dirty shallow chimney and then up a short rake to a rock corner on the left.

1 30 feet. Ascend the wall above for about 10 feet and then move over the edge on the right, cross the slab to a bracket on the next ridge and move round into a chimney with a good belay.

2 50 feet. Climb the rather difficult chimney, (avoiding a large poised block at the top), to a grass ledge. Enter the unusual rock cavity on the right and ascend to a ledge with block belays.

3 35 feet. Go up the overhanging crack in the corner above to a big block belay.

4 55 feet. A little crack on the left is followed by easy climbing to a ledge directly above the chimney of pitch 2.

5 65 feet. A pleasant easy ridge leads to a gap before a steep wall.

6 35 feet. Go down into the gap, up the gendarme and over a stride to a good stance. Walk along the ridge to a second gap.

7 25 feet. Descend the vertical wall. This pitch, which is severe, may be abseiled.

8 45 feet. Go up the easy opposite side of the gap bearing left.

9 50 feet. An easy ridge is climbed to a small spike belay at the foot of cracks.

10 20 feet. Go up the cracks to a large block belay.

11 20 feet. Now ascend the final wall to the summit.

'D' Gully. Moderate.
This is the wide gully to the left of Mare's Nest Buttress and contains a cave pitch, which is usually wet.

Horse and Man Rock

This is the shattered tower forming the left wall of 'D' Gully. The lower part is very broken. The easiest line is over ledges on the right, then across to a recess. A grassy groove follows and is climbed for 40 feet. An easy traverse to the left is then taken round two corners to the foot of a line of chimneys. Four short pitches lead to a cave, which is left by a tortuous hole almost 20 feet high. A little scrambling follows.

Steeplechase. 375 feet. Severe (mild).
Runs from the foot of 'D' Gully up Horse and Man Buttress. Scrappy and contrived in its lower parts, but improving somewhat as it progresses, it starts from the bed of the gully about 50 feet down from a large overhanging block. A cracked wall rises on the left and the climb begins at its left-hand end.

1 65 feet. Climb directly up the wall; then traverse to the right to approach a loose block. Continue up the wall above this, bearing left to a grass ledge. Move back to the right and up an easy ridge to a large block belay.

2 30 feet. Move right and follow the easy ridge to block belays near a steep rib.

3 70 feet. Climb the crest of the rib to a grass traverse. Walk left for 20 feet to a grassy corner and then climb the easy slabs on the left to a ledge and belays.

4 45 feet. Go straight up the edge of the rib to a bilberry ledge and belay.

5 70 feet. Ascend the vertical corner straight above; then bear leftwards up slabs to the edge of a chimney. Go up the chimney for a few feet, then a groove on the right wall and finally a steep little face on the right. Move back to the left to a chockstone belay at the top of the chimney.

6 30 feet. Climb the steep wall on the left and traverse on to the arête. Belays.

7 30 feet. Easy climbing up the pleasant arête.

8 35 feet. The ridge ahead is climbed to the Horse and Man cairn.

The remaining gullies, 'C', 'B' and 'A', are not worth climbing except under winter conditions.

'C' Gully. Moderate.
There is only one pitch.

'B' Gully. Difficult (hard).
Scrambling alternates with short pitches, a difficult chimney leading to a large cave being the main obstacle.

'A' Gully. Moderate.
Scrambling leads to a green mossy chimney in a corner on the right or another chimney on the left: both have awkward finishes.

Western Buttress. 130 feet. Very difficult.
This is the left wall of 'A' Gully.

1 75 feet. Start in the middle of a steep wall. Work slightly right, then left and over a steepening of the rock. Easier climbing to the right leads to a large ledge and block belay.

2 15 feet. Step off the block and climb a crack to the left. Terrace, belay.

3 40 feet. Go up a little crack on the left and walk to the right up a glacis to the cairn.
The climb can be extended by scrambling in the same line above the final pitch for 50 feet to reach a spike-belay. Traverse to the right to the edge of 'A' gully and finish up the edge of the steep nose on good holds.

ESK BUTTRESS (223065)

The Approaches

Marked on the map as Dow Crag, Esk Buttress is set in splendid isolation on the south-east spur of Scafell Pike, overlooking Upper Eskdale. From Taw House in Eskdale, which is the natural starting point for Esk Buttress, a 2-hour walk following the Esk Hause track leads to the foot of the crag, and takes in some of the wildest and most delightful scenery in the district.
From Wasdale the normal track to Mickledore is taken, followed by a descent via Cam Spout. 2 hours.

From Borrowdale, the path up Grain Ghyll leads to Esk Hause and so down into upper Eskdale in 2½ hours.
From Langdale, if transport is available, it is best to drive to Cockley Beck, from where an easy, though often wet, walk up Mosedale leads to Lingcove Beck. Contour below Long Crag and Gait Crags (indeterminate track) to arrive at Esk Buttress in 1½ hours from Cockley Beck. If no transport is available, the shortest route lies via Three Tarns. Contour below Bowfell Links and cross Yeastyrigg Crags. About 2½ hours.

Topographical

Although traditionally known as a buttress, this is a crag in its own right, the magnificent Central Pillar giving some of the longest and finest routes in the district. When the higher crags are wet and cheerless, it is worth remembering that Esk Buttress faces south-east and, due to its lower altitude (1,500 feet), it can often be found in perfect condition.
The main feature of the crag is the Central Pillar, bounded on the left by the deep chimney of Frustration and on the right by the angular corner of Trespasser Groove. Beyond the chimney of Frustration is the open corner of Gargoyle Stairs, the Gargoyle peering over its left-bounding wall.
To the right of Trespasser Groove the crag becomes easier-angled at the point where Bower's Route breaks through, before steepening again and merging into the wall of the deeply-cut Left Esk Chimney.
Below the central mass of the crag is a sub-structure of broken rock and vegetation, which makes the starts of climbs difficult to locate. Once the preliminary scrambling is over however, the lines become quite obvious, often appallingly so !
The best way of descent from the summit is by striking across to a stream, which skirts the left-hand side of the crag (true right).
The climbs are described from left to right.

Afterthought. 90 feet. Severe.

A pleasant route to finish off the day in the evening sun. Lies up a steep cracked wall on the left end of the crag overlooking the stream. Cairn.

1 40 feet. The crack above the cairn gives steep climbing to a stance and huge belay.

2 50 feet. Continue straight up the steep rocks above to the top.

Moss. 180 feet. Very severe (mild).

Starts 30 feet left of Gargoyle Groove, a perched block high up on the mossy wall being the most obvious feature.

1 30 feet. Ascend an easy rightward-sloping ramp. Belay on lodged blocks.

2 150 feet. Step right, and climb the overhanging arête. Continue up towards the perched block, move to the right a few feet below it, and climb the groove to a good ledge. Step right, and climb the arête to the top.

Gargoyle Groove. 185 feet. Very severe.

A pleasant climb giving much better climbing than its apparently broken and lichenous appearance would suggest. The route lies up a well-defined groove slanting up to the right and terminating on the immediate left of the Gargoyle. Its easy appearance from below is probably due to the contrast with the blank wall on the right. Starts at the foot of a small buttress directly below the groove.

1 65 feet. Climb the buttress to a large sloping bilberry ledge. Large belay on the left.

2 60 feet. Climb up the groove over doubtful blocks until forced on to the left wall by an overhanging nose in the centre of the groove. After a few feet of steep and strenuous ascent, an awkward move is made to the right to attain the tip of the nose above the overhang, when easier climbing leads to a massive pinnacle belay on the left.

3 60 feet. Continue straight up the groove to the top, a fairly high standard of difficulty being maintained throughout.

Gargoyle Direct. 290 feet. Very severe.
A very pleasant climb. Starts directly below the Gargoyle at the lowest point of the buttress between Gargoyle Groove and Gargoyle Stairs. The principal pitch goes up the steep wall to the right of the Gargoyle before traversing left on to the rib bounding the right-hand side of Gargoyle Groove.

1 120 feet. Easy climbing up the buttress to the large bilberry ledge, passing a dead tree *en route.*

2 40 feet. From the left-hand end of the ledge scramble up to the heather ledges below the steep wall and follow these to the centre of the wall where a small spike belay will be found.

3 130 feet. Move left along the ledge, then climb the wall above to a large good spike then move to the right to a long sloping ledge. Climb the steep crack for 15 feet and move to a resting place on the left. Continue left on to the rib and climb this on substantial holds, passing a good spike, until a difficult balance move leads to a ledge below the Gargoyle. Ascend the short crack on the left and belay on a large block at the top.

Grand Slam. 290 feet. Extremely severe.
An airy and enjoyable climb, the main pitch giving steep, strenuous climbing of increasing difficulty. Starts as for Gargoyle Direct.

1 120 feet. As for Gargoyle Direct.

2 30 feet. As for pitch 2 of Boot Hill.

3 20 feet. Climb on to the pinnacle above; then move left to the heather ledge. (Spike belay below a line of thin cracks).

4 90 feet. Climb directly behind the belay for about 40 feet until the crack disappears. Move diagonally up to the right for a few feet; then go up to beneath the large overhang. Pull round the overhang and climb the wall, with difficulty, to a ledge in the groove. Belays.

5 30 feet. Climb the groove to the top.

Boot Hill. 280 feet. Very severe (hard).

A pleasant climb, which follows the shallow groove line 40 feet right of Gargoyle Direct.

1 120 feet. As for Gargoyle Direct.

2 30 feet. Traverse 30 feet to the right, along the bilberry ledge, to a large pinnacle directly below the groove.

3 100 feet. Climb the pinnacle and groove above. Continue up the steep groove; then on big holds ascend to a small ledge and belay.

4 30 feet. Climb the crack to an awkward finish.

Gargoyle's Stairs. 290 feet. Severe (hard).

Follows the line of a dirty corner, which runs up to the right of the Gargoyle. It provides interesting climbing but is spoiled somewhat by vegetation. Starts almost directly beneath the Gargoyle at a crevassed block. Cairn.

1 30 feet. A rib just to the right of the cairn is followed to a detached block belay.

2 40 feet. Continue up the rib to a stance and small belay.

3 50 feet. A steep grassy slope leads up to a right-angled corner of reddish rock.

4 40 feet. The corner is climbed with some difficulty, chiefly due to its steepness as the holds are good. A small stance and spike belay are reached.

5 50 feet. Follow the grassy groove above to a good ledge and small spike belay.

6 60 feet. Continue up the groove to a stance and spike belay.

7 20 feet. The top is attained with no further difficulty.

West Point. 225 feet. Extremely severe.

The route, which climbs the wall to the right of the main corner of Gargoyle Stairs, starts from the large grass slope 30 feet below, and to the right of the top of pitch 3 of that climb.

1 50 feet. Move into the shallow corner and climb it, round an overhang, to a sloping ledge. Traverse right for 10 feet; then move up to a small overhang, pull over this, and climb up to a small stance and piton belay (in place).

2 65 feet. Climb straight above the belay for 20 feet to a ledge; then move diagonally left to a shallow groove in the arête. Climb the groove to a nut belay beside a large poised block, (junction with pitch 7 of Frustration).

3 110 feet. A good pitch. From the top of the block, step left and up, using side holds, to a line of small flakes. Climb up steeply to a narrow ledge below a shallow corner. Climb the groove for a few feet to the overhang; then move left on to the wall. Pull over the overhang into another corner, which eases after a few feet and leads more easily to the top.

Frustration. 315 feet. Severe (hard).

The route starts up the well-defined chimney to the left of the Central Pillar, but the difficulties of the upper crag enforce a long excursion out to the left for a finish. Starts below the foot of the chimney.

1 40 feet. Steep rocks lead to the foot of the chimney. Belay low down on the left.

2 50 feet. Climb the chimney until an exit can be made out to the left to a good ledge and belay.

3 50 feet. The wall above is climbed near its right-hand edge for about 15 feet, when a short traverse left is made to a line of good holds leading straight up to a grass ledge. There is a good belay on a small rock ledge a few feet higher.

4 30 feet. Climb grassy rocks to a juniper bush and a belay in a corner just to the right.

5 20 feet. A step up to the right is made on to a rock gangway, which is followed to the left to a belay at the foot of a steep crack.

6 20 feet. Descend diagonally to the left for 10 feet, step round the corner on the left and then descend again to a grass ledge and belay.

7 40 feet. Descend a few feet and traverse to the left, passing beneath a pinnacle, which is loose and should be avoided. Move round a corner to enter a shallow, grassy chimney (Gargoyle's Stairs) ; a few feet up the chimney is a small ledge and belay.

8 25 feet. A rising traverse left leads to another small ledge and a juniper belay.

9 40 feet. Ascend a crack for a few feet until level with the top of a small pinnacle on the left; then traverse to the right for 10 feet and ascend directly to the top.

Variation Finish. **Satisfaction.** 85 feet. Very severe (hard). This route follows the natural continuation of the climb up the steep crack above pitch 5 of the normal route and is considerably more difficult.

6a 55 feet. Climb the crack, with difficulty, for about 20 feet then traverse left on to the exposed buttress until upward progress becomes possible. Move back right to a spike belay and poor stance.

7a 30 feet. Straight up the groove above.

Amoeba. 265 feet. Very severe (hard).
This route follows a line parallel to, and just left of Red Edge, and is, in fact, the direct continuation of Frustration chimney.

1 90 feet. Pitches 1 and 2 of Frustration.

2 60 feet. Climb the steep crack on the right side of the chimney to a grass ledge on the left. Pull out, awkwardly, to a stance.

3 70 feet. Traverse right and climb the steep groove and crack continuation to the pile of flakes on Bridge's Route (top of pitch 7).

4 45 feet. Climb the mossy groove above to the top, as for Bridge's Route, pitch 8.

The Red Edge. 240 feet. Very severe (hard).
A bold and exposed climb following a very striking line up the steep shallow groove in the left-bounding rib of the steep wall of the Central Pillar. It is actually the right-hand arête of the chimney of Frustration. Starts as for Frustration.

1 40 feet. Steep rocks lead to the foot of the chimney. Belay low down on the left.

2 130 feet. Ascend the chimney for 15 feet until a thin short flake-crack in its right wall leads up to the rib. The shallow groove ahead is climbed until, at about 85 feet, a small square-cut overhang bars the way. Pull over the overhang into a groove. After a few feet the groove, which deepens and becomes easier with a good crack in the back, leads to a grassy stance and belay on the right.

3 70 feet. Move up and to the left, more easily, and ascend the arête to the top.

Hydra. 200 feet. Extremely severe.
A technical and interesting climb, which ascends the shallow, hanging groove in the wall to the right of The Red Edge. Scramble up to the steep section of the wall, (flake belays).

1 130 feet. Climb diagonally left on to the arête (very close to Red Edge), and move up under a bulge to a good ledge level with the foot of the groove. Move to the right into the groove, and climb it using one piton near the top. Step right; then climb up and left to a juniper ledge. Climb the continuation of the groove to the stance on Red Edge.

2 70 feet. Climb the short corner and wall on the left, on big holds, to the top.

Black Sunday. 305 feet. Very severe (hard).
A good climb, best attempted in dry conditions owing to some mossy sections. Follows the obvious crack and groove line between the Red Edge and Square Chimney. Starts at the foot of the arête, which runs down from the Red Edge.

1 95 feet. Easy climbing up the arête to a bilberry ledge and ash belay.

2 20 feet. Up to a belay below, and to the left of the prominent bulging mossy crack.

3 90 feet. Climb the overhanging crack and make an awkward exit on to a glacis on the right (running belay). Move back into the crack, which is climbed for a few feet until it narrows. Make a long stride to the left to a thin slanting crack, which is climbed to a good resting place under the overhang. Traverse back right to the crack and pull awkwardly, round the overhang on to the wall on the right, where good holds lead up to a rock ledge and belay. (Instead of making the long stride to the left and the traverse back right, it is possible to climb straight up the crack. This involves a difficult layback move and a hard pull on a sod and is not recommended).

4 55 feet. Climb straight up the corner-crack above; the difficulties ease at 30 feet when more broken rocks lead up to a stance and belay on the left.

5 45 feet. Above is a mossy scoop. Climb the wall on the left of the scoop to the top. Belay 30 feet back on the terrace.

Square Chimney Route. 315 feet. Very severe.
An excellent route with fine situations. The Square Chimney is easily identified on the wall of the Central Pillar to the right of the Red Edge. The climb finishes at the foot of the final tower but, by adding the last 3 pitches of Medusa Wall, a pleasant extension is provided. Starts up the arête, which runs down from the Red Edge.

1 35 feet. Easy climbing up the arête. Stance and belay.

2 35 feet. Go straight up to another belay.

3 30 feet. Continue to a bilberry ledge and ash belay.

4 45 feet. Traverse right until directly below the square chimney; then climb up to a stance and juniper belay at its foot.

5 40 feet. Climb the chimney by the back and foot method. (It is rather too wide for comfort for the average climber). An awkward exit is made on to a tiny sloping ledge at the top of the chimney on its left. Small flake belay at waist level and a much better one 10 feet higher. This is best approached by stepping across the chimney into the corner-crack and climbing up it for a few feet.

6 50 feet. Traverse delicately left across a mossy slab to enter an open mossy groove with a crack in the corner. This is ascended on fairly good holds to a small but comfortable stance and belay.

7 30 feet. Continue, either up the groove or up the arête on the left, to a sloping ledge at the end of the traverse on Bridge's Route. Stance and belay on the ledge a few feet higher on the left.

8 50 feet. Step up to the right into the bed of a shallow gully, which gives pleasant climbing to the top of the crag.

Medusa Wall. 440 feet. Very severe.

A fine climb, sharing some of its early pitches with Square Chimney and Bridge's Route before continuing up the exposed edge of the final tower of the Central Pillar. Starts directly below the Square Chimney.

1 115 feet. Rock and steep vegetation lead to a stance and juniper belay below the chimney.

2 60 feet. The chimney is climbed for some 15 feet when a large flat foothold on the right wall can be attained. The crack just to the right is then climbed for 10 feet when it peters out, and is followed by a short traverse left to another crack in the corner. This is ascended, holds on the left wall proving useful, to the ledge above pitch 4 of Bridge's Route.

3 45 feet. (Pitch 5 of Bridge's Route). The steep groove above leads to a jammed spike of rock. A short traverse to the right is then made followed by a direct ascent on good holds to a good ledge and belay.

4 40 feet. (Pitch 6 of Bridge's Route). Traverse left to a mossy ledge; then climb the left-hand groove to a stance and belay (Square Chimney Route is rejoined here).

5 40 feet. Climb up the gully and then out to the right to a rock ledge below the final tower. Belay on the left.

6 45 feet. Climb the central one of three main grooves above the belay to the top of a pinnacle; then move round to the right and up to a good stance and belay on the edge of the tower.

7 30 feet. Start up the groove containing the belay and, after 15 feet, move to the right on to the rib and up to a large bilberry and juniper ledge. Belay.

8 65 feet. Easy climbing, diagonally right, is followed by scrambling to the top.

Bridge's Route. 410 feet. Severe (hard).
One of the two original climbs on the crag (the other being Bower's), which are now deservedly classics. They combine varied and interesting climbing with considerable length and exposure. The start is best located by going 60 feet left from the right-hand toe of the buttress and scrambling up for 50 feet, on the left of a grassy bay, to the foot of a slabby rib. Spikes up on the right are a landmark.

1 90 feet. Slabs with good holds lead to a wide ledge. Belay.

2 80 feet. Ascend a little buttress on the right of a mossy hollow; then traverse diagonally upwards over grass to the left and climb up past two ledges to a recess with a belay.

3 45 feet. The steep rocks straight ahead are climbed, with deviations to right and left, following the best line of holds. A grass ledge is reached and a belay suitable for a sitting position.

4 25 feet. Climb the crack on the left and follow the flake to a ledge and belay.

5 45 feet. Enter the steep groove above and climb it to the level of a jammed spike; move right and climb straight up on good holds to a ledge and large belay.

6 40 feet. Traverse left to a mossy ledge and then climb the left-hand groove to a stance and belay.

7 40 feet. Descend a little from the stance and then make a slightly ascending traverse left to a pile of flakes on the corner of the buttress. Small belay.

8 45 feet. The steep mossy groove, slightly on the right, has good holds and leads, in 20 feet, to a grassy shelf with a belay at its upper extremity.

The Central Pillar. 495 feet. Extremely severe.
A magnificent climb taking the obvious but intimidating line up the face of the final tower. The first four pitches are shared with Bridge's Route. Start as for Bridge's Route.

1 90 feet. Slabs with good holds are climbed to a ledge. Belay.

2 80 feet. Ascend the little buttress on the right of a mossy hollow; then traverse diagonally upwards over grass to the left and climb up past two ledges to a recess with belay.

3 70 feet. The steep rocks straight ahead are climbed with deviations right and left, following the best line of holds to a grass ledge. Climb the crack on the left and follow the flake to a ledge and belay.

4 45 feet. Step left and climb the steep groove past a jammed spike, move right and climb up to a good ledge and belay.

5 70 feet. Climb up for a few feet to a good inserted chockstone. Traverse diagonally right until the rock gets steeper; then step round a nose to a ledge with small flake belays.

6 40 feet. Climb the steep rocks above, make an awkward move over a bulge; then move right and up mossy slabs to a spike high up on the left (piton belay in place).

7 70 feet. Traverse to the right under the steep wall and move up to a very small ledge. Move left, protected by a piton, over a large block and up the wall above to a narrow ledge which leads to the right to a grassy bay.

8 30 feet. Up the wide crack on the left or, better, the one on the right of the bay.

Great Central Climb. 525 feet. Very severe.
A fine route, which goes up the lower part of the face of the Central Pillar before being forced out to the right from near the foot of the final tower, to finish up Bower's Route. Starts below the middle of the Central Pillar.

1 100 feet. Scramble up to a conspicuous grass ledge.

2 80 feet. Climb straight up rocks and vegetation to where a pinnacle leans against the face at the foot of the Central Pillar proper.

3 50 feet. From the top of the pinnacle, move up diagonally to the right, then up to finish on three perched blocks on the immediate right of a small overhanging nose. Belay.

4 35 feet. A delicate traverse is made to the left, under the nose, to enter a groove, which is ascended to a small ledge. The wall above is climbed and the large ledge on the left attained by a mantelshelf move. Belay. 10 feet above.

5 40 feet. Climb up until it is possible to use the belay as a foothold. After a delicate traverse to the right towards the edge of the buttress, climb the wall above to a small recess and belay.

6 20 feet. Ascend the left-hand of two grooves above until an obvious traverse line leads towards the edge of the rib on the right. Using small holds, move round the rib and attain a small ledge in the large groove (Trespasser Groove). Spike belay.

7 50 feet. The abseil. Using the belay spike (or alternatively a piton if in place and trustworthy), abseil some 15 feet down the groove to assume a bridging position. (It is possible to climb down this section). Move out to the right, surmount a grass ledge and ascend to another grass ledge 10 feet higher. An inconspicuous natural thread belay is low down on the left.

8 30 feet. Climb straight up to a comfortable juniper ledge. Belay at the left end.

9 40 feet. Climb up the overhanging crack above the middle of the ledge, then up to the Waiting Room on Bower's Route. Frankland's Crack is immediately above.

10 50 feet. The slightly overhanging crack gives strenuous climbing with an awkward finish. Easy slab then lead leftwards to a chockstone belay on the right of a steep crack.

11 30 feet. The crack, steep and rather strenuous, completes the climb.

Variation. The Direct Route. Very severe (hard).

7a 40 feet. From the spike belay in Trespasser Groove, move up and make an awkward mantelshelf move on to a narrow ledge on the right wall of the groove. The steep wall above is split by a thin crack, which curves to the left; this provides the main handhold for a very awkward ascent to a good flake about 15 feet above. From the flake traverse right without difficulty, over doubtful blocks, to a good ledge and large belays.

8a 40 feet. From the right-hand end of the ledge, ascend a groove; then continue up to the Waiting Room to rejoin the original route.

Tresspasser Groove. 435 feet. Very severe (hard).
The route trespasses on to Bower's Route for both start and finish and, in between, follows the conspicuous corner bounding the Central Pillar on its right. Despite the lack of independence, the line of the route is a natural one and the climbing is both interesting and hard. Start as for Bower's Route.

1 100 feet. The slabs are climbed from left to right, finishing along a grassy shelf to a sloping heather terrace. Belay round a block.

2 35 feet. Make a diagonal upward traverse left to a small ledge and belay.

3 50 feet. A groove slanting up to the right, a little to the right of the belay, leads to grass ledges and a poor belay at the foot of a groove. It is advisable to insert a piton for a belay at this point.

4 90 feet. Move up the slab, then across left to enter the groove in the corner; ascend it on small but adequate holds to a recess (nut runner). The bulge above is overcome by the use of holds on the right wall to enter another recess (runner). The awkward bulge above is then climbed by bridging, facing left, until holds can be attained for the pull-up into the recess below the Director Route on Great Central Climb. Spike belay.

5 40 feet. An awkward mantelshelf move on to a ledge on the right wall of the groove is followed by hard climbing up the wall above to a flake (runner). A traverse can then be made to a good ledge on the right. Large belays.

6 40 feet. Climb the corner on the left to the overhang and make a very long reach out to the right to a small handhold. Swing across on this and ascend, on good holds, to the Waiting Room on Bower's Route.

7 50 feet. Frankland's Crack. The slightly overhanging crack gives strenuous climbing with an awkward finish. Easy slabs then lead leftwards to a bay and chockstone belay on the right of a steep crack. On the right of the bay is another crack.

8 30 feet. The crack on the right, steep and rather strenuous with some undercut layback moves, completes the climb.

Bower's Route. 415 feet. Severe (hard).
An excellent route, the first on the buttress to be ascended. Starts below a sweep of slabs reached by going 60 feet to the left, up an easy slanting rake, from the scree at the right-hand side of the main crag.

1 100 feet. The slabs are climbed from left to right, finishing along a grassy shelf, to a sloping heather terrace. Block belay.

2 35 feet. Make a diagonal upward traverse to the left to a small ledge and belay.

3 60 feet. A groove slanting up to the right, a little to the right of the belay, leads to grass ledges and a belay at the foot of a steep crack.

4 60 feet. The crack is climbed on good holds, starting just on its left and finishing to the right, on to some ledges. A belay is reached in a corner, back to the left above the crack.

5 50 feet. The very steep rocks above are followed by a nose. A traverse left then leads to the Waiting Room. Belays.

6 20 feet. Climb a severe chimney, which starts from the right-hand end of the ledge, above the right wall of the Waiting Room. Small belays.

7 30 feet. The V-chimney. Break out on the right to a perfect rock ledge with a flake belay high up.

8 60 feet. Climb the slabs on the right which soon become easy.

Variation. Kirkus's alternative to pitch 6.

6a 35 feet. Instead of the vertical chimney, the wall on its right is traversed for 10 feet, passing a doubtful cube of rock. A flake runs back diagonally left to the belay at the top of the chimney. (The traverse is delicate and the flake strenuous).

Variation. Frankland's Finish. Very severe.

6b 50 feet. The slightly overhanging crack immediately above the Waiting Room gives strenuous climbing with an awkward finish. Easy slabs then lead leftwards to a bay and a chockstone belay on the right of a steep crack (the left one).

7b 30 feet. The crack on the left, steep and rather strenuous, completes the climb.

Serpent Route. 375 feet. Severe (hard).

The route runs up the wall on the right of Bower's Route, which it joins for the finish. Starts immediately right of the foot of the rake leading to Bower's Route, below the steep face on the left of the Esk Chimneys.

1 40 feet. Slabs above a cairn are followed by a broken groove and lead, without difficulty, to a belay.

2 60 feet. Steep and awkward climbing straight up from the belay gives access to a large grassy shelf in about 40 feet; at the back of the shelf, 20 feet higher, there is a good belay.

3 35 feet. Climb up to the overhang above the belay, make a difficult step to the right; then go straight up to a small ledge below a crack. Flake belay high up on the left.

4 25 feet. Climb the crack until it is possible to step out to a ledge. Continue straight up to a stance and belay.

5 40 feet. Climb the steep rib on the left to join the crack on Bower's Route. Continue to the belay at the top of pitch 4 of Bower's Route, which is now followed.

6 50 feet. The very steep rocks above are followed by a nose. A traverse is then made to the left to the Waiting Room.

7 35 feet. Instead of climbing the vertical chimney, traverse the wall on its right for 10 feet, passing a doubtful cube of rock. A flake running back diagonally to the left is followed to a belay at the top of the chimney. (The traverse is delicate and the flake strenuous—Kirkus's Variation to Bower's Route).

8 30 feet. The V-chimney. Break out on the right to a perfect rock ledge with a flake belay high up.

9 60 feet. Climb the slabs on the right, which soon become easy.

Right-Hand Route. 335 feet. Very severe (hard).
A route up the wall to the right of Serpent. Starts in a recess about 20 feet right of Serpent below an obvious overhanging crack at 60 feet.

1 40 feet. Climb the corner-crack to a small stance and belay below the overhanging crack.

2 50 feet. Ascend the overhanging crack to a large terrace. Belay at a pair of junipers at the back of the terrace.

3 60 feet. Step off a block lying against the face, and climb the small overhang by layback (the crux). Continue up for a few feet, then traverse right and up to a large ledge and large flake belay.

4 90 feet. Go round the corner on the left to another belay. Make a semi-hand-traverse back right to gain a shallow groove on the rib, and follow this to easier ground at 40 feet. Climb up rocky ledges to a grass ledge below a steep wall. Walk round the corner on the right to belay below a steep corner-crack.

5 95 feet. Climb up the crack to the overhang (strenuous). Step left and go up to a steep corner above. Gain a small ledge in the corner then traverse across the right wall and up to the top of the crag.

Variation. Direct Finish 80 feet. Very severe (hard).
Starts from the grass ledge, which is reached on pitch 4 of

Right-Hand Route. This is below and to the right of the chimney (pitch 6) of Bower's Route.

80 feet. Start about 12 feet right of the corner and make a hard pull-up to a line of flake holds leading up to the right. Follow these to a small stance on the rib and go round the corner on the right into a groove. Pull over an overhang and climb the groove to the top.

Variation. Flake Climb 180 feet. Very severe (mild).
Starting from the top of pitch 3 of Right Hand Route the flake crack runs up the right-hand side of the buttress and finishes in the gully.

The Girdle Traverse. 570 feet. Very severe.
An excellent route with some good situations, which follows a good line right across the main part of the crag. It gives very good climbing without a high standard of difficulty. Previous knowledge of the topography of the crag is advisable. Start as for Frustration.

1 40 feet. Steep rocks lead to the foot of the chimney. Belay low down on the left.

2 50 feet. Climb the chimney until an exit can be made out to the left to a good ledge and belay.

3 50 feet. The wall above is climbed near its right-hand edge for about 15 feet when a short traverse left is made to a line of holds leading straight up to a grass ledge. There is a good belay on a small rock ledge a few feet higher.

4 55 feet. The Red Wall. Traverse a few feet to the right; then climb the steep wall towards an overhang until a good spike is reached (runner); traverse the wall to make a landing on the obvious small ledge on the right. Climb diagonally to the right, on good holds, to a good juniper ledge and belays.

5 45 feet. Climb the short crack above and traverse along a juniper ledge to a rock ledge and belay. (Junction with pitch 6 of Bridge's Route).

6 40 feet. Descend a groove for 10 feet; then follow the obvious traverse line to the right to a ledge and block belay. (Pitch 6 of Bridge's Route reversed).

7 70 feet. Traverse some 10 feet to the right; then descend until it is possible to make a delicate traverse across a wall on the right. (Junction with Great Central Route). Continue the traverse to reach the edge of the buttress; then climb the wall to a recess in a groove. Another recess is reached 15 feet higher, (belay 15 feet up on the left).

7a An alternative line, after the initial traverse of 10 feet to the right, ascends the wall above for 20 feet then goes to the right to a ledge. Belay at the right-hand end of the ledge; then descend to the stance as above.

8 20 feet. Ascend the left one of two grooves for 10 feet. Traverse to the right to the edge of the rib; then move round it, on small holds, to a small ledge in Trespasser Groove. (Pitch 7, Great Central Route). Small spike belay or piton belay.

9 50 feet. Descend slightly to attain a foothold under the lip of the shelving ledge, which forms the stance; then step across to the right, on to the wall, which is traversed to attain good holds. (If necessary the last man can use a doubled sling through the belay piton in order to start this move). Go past grass ledges and climb, easily, straight up to a comfortable juniper ledge with a good belay at the left end.

10 40 feet. Climb up the overhanging crack above the middle of the ledge and ascend to the Waiting Room on Bower's Route.

11 110 feet. From the right-hand edge of the ledge, a vertical chimney runs upwards (Pitch 6 of Bower's Route). Traverse the wall on the right of the chimney for 15 feet, passing a doubtful piece of rock. Traverse to the right, and slightly downwards round a corner, passing below a steep groove to reach the foot of a second groove. Climb the groove, slightly leftwards, to a mantelshelf ledge; then move diagonally right to attain the nose. Follow this upwards until the angle eases and easy ground is reached.

Esk Chimneys

These are the two deeply-cut vertical chimneys on the right of the Esk Buttress. Each is about 40 feet high and hardly worthy of attention.

Wall Finish. 110 feet. Severe.

About 40 feet above the point where Esk Chimneys join, there is a pile of large blocks at the foot of a 40-foot slab on the left wall. The route starts here.

1 60 feet. Traverse left across the slab and go up the arête to a grassy ledge. Traverse left again to the foot of a 15-foot corner-crack.

2 50 feet. Climb the crack to a grass ledge. In the far corner is another grass ledge. Gain it and pull over to the top.

Chimney Buttress. 225 feet. Very difficult.

The climb follows the rib on the right of the left Esk Chimney.

1 90 feet. Climb up the rib, which is steep at first but eases at 50 feet. Easier climbing then leads to a stance and belay where the rib steepens again.

2 40 feet. From the belay climb straight up to a juniper ledge. Small belay high up.

3 25 feet. Steep rock is climbed, slightly right, to another juniper ledge. Block belay a few feet left.

4 40 feet. A steep groove at the right-hand end of the ledge is climbed to a small stance with a perfect flake belay.

5 30 feet. Climb the obvious groove to the overhanging blocks, which are climbed on the right, to a boulder-strewn ledge. Scrambling leads to the top of the buttress.

Some 200 yards to the right of Esk Buttress, and on the same contour, is a small crag split by a gigantic cleft; on it are two short climbs.

Thor's Cave. 100 feet. Severe (mild).

The start is reached by walking up the bed of the cleft to the foot of an obvious cave pitch.

1 25 feet. Ascend to a small cave and constricted stance. Small spike belay on the left inside the cave.

2 25 feet. This pitch looks much worse than it is. The overhang is climbed by backing up, facing left. Thread belay.

3 50 feet. From a little higher up the bed of the cleft, traverse out on the left wall to the lower of two chockstones. Mount the higher and larger chockstone to finish on top of the crag.

Thunder Rib. 120 feet. Very difficult.

The climb follows the rib to the right of the entrance to Thor's Cave.

1 15 feet. The rib is climbed to a block.

2 25 feet. Bear slightly right up overhanging blocks to a good ledge and block belay.

3 30 feet. Climb up to the grassy corner. Large spike belay.

4 50 feet. The chimney is climbed to the top.

ROUGH CRAG (217071)

Facing east across the head of Little Narrowcove is a considerable area of rock split by a deep-cut scree gully. On the right of the gully is a steep but rather broken face with a detached pinnacle, and on the left is a well defined ridge culminating in a steep tower. The rock is inclined to be dirty and has outward sloping holds, but in dry conditions the ridge gives an interesting climb.

Narrowcove Buttress. 250 feet. Severe.

Gain the crest of the rock ridge from just right of the base, and climb via short corners and cracks to the platform with block belays below the steep final tower (200 feet). A line of holds slants leftwards, across the wall, to reach a groove, which leads up past some loose blocks to finish on grass ledges (50 feet).
There is an alternative to the last pitch.

Direct Finish. 60 feet. Severe (hard).

Behind belays, just right of centre, is a shallow corner, which is climbed on awkward sloping holds until it is possible to traverse left on a small ledge to a break. Ascend this, and go rightwards to the top.

GREAT END, ESK PIKE AND LINGMELL

GREAT END (228085)

The crags of Great End cover almost the whole of the north-east face of the mountain and overlook Sprinkling Tarn and the Sty Head, Esk Hause track. From the right-hand end of the crag, a broad ridge runs down to Sty Head with the deep gully of Skew Ghyll on its right. This gully makes an interesting route to the summit in winter when combined with Cust's Gully.

The crag is scarcely worth a visit in summer but it gives excellent winter climbing and is in condition more often than any other face in the Lake District, with the possible exception of the eastern side of Helvellyn.

The climbs are described from left to right.

Brigg's Climb. 40 feet. Difficult.

A great cave, spanned by an enormous chockstone, near the left end of the crag. Climb the wall on the right of the cave to a ledge and belay at 20 feet. A crack on the right of the belay follows.

Brothers' Crack. 95 feet. Very difficult.

Starts in a well-marked corner about 50 yards to the right of Brigg's Climb. A scramble leads to the foot of the corner.

1 20 feet. A 10-foot corner leads to a ledge and a further corner to a belay.

2 35 feet. Continue up the crack to a good belay below a cave.

3 25 feet. The cave is difficult to enter and is followed by a difficult crack. Good belay but poor stance in the crack.

4 15 feet. An overhanging finish with good holds.

Wayfarer's Crack. Severe (mild).

A 40-foot pitch up a corner, a little to the left of the finish of Brothers' Crack.

Great End Gullies

The two obvious gullies near the centre of the crag are respectively, South-East Gully and Central Gully. Large quantities of loose scree between pitches render them unpleasant in summer when their grade is moderate. A few notes on winter conditions may be of assistance.

South-East Gully. 600 feet.

With a big build-up of ice, this is the harder of the two gullies. An ice pitch at 200 feet can be avoided by traversing right and rejoining the gully immediately above it.

Central Gully. 600 feet.

This varies considerably with conditions. The crux is at the point where the gully forks (the right fork being the normal route) and a 10-foot ice pitch or alternatively an easy snow slope, may be found. The summit cornice is sometimes considerable and the upper part of the gully has been known to avalanche on occasions.

Cust's Gully.

This is well up towards the right-hand end of the crag and easily identified by a huge chockstone forming an arch. It is useful as a way down after ascending the other gullies.

Stand Crag (219088)

A small crag on Great End just to the left of (true right), and level with the main fall of Greta Ghyll.

Rowan Tree Buttress. 150 feet.

A broken stretch of rock near the left side of the crag.

Little Buttress. 100 feet. Difficult.

A slabby buttress near the middle of the face, just to the left of a grassy gully.

1 40 feet. A traverse to the left is taken and the route goes up the centre of a slab to a stance on its left edge. Belay.
2 40 feet. After a step round to the left, follow the left edge of the face to a stance and belay.
3 20 feet. Finishing directly is a grade harder than the other pitches but it may be avoided.

All Sorts. 125 feet. Severe (mild).

Starts just to the right of Little Buttress at the lowest point of the crag.
1 40 feet. Climb the short steep wall to a grassy groove. Stance and belay in the corner.
2 85 feet. Traverse to the right to the arête and ascend this direct by pleasant climbing to a knife-edge. The groove on the right leads to easier climbing and the top of the crag.

Eros. 120 feet. Very difficult.

Starts 25 feet to the left of South Face Route at the foot of a steep wall.
1 50 feet. Climb the wall and follow the easier slab to a large stance at the foot of a steep overhanging wall. Step left and follow the gully to a block belay.
2 70 feet. Climb the steep arête on the right to a delicate finish on a grass ledge.

South Face Route. 105 feet. Severe.

Starts just on the right of a big V-groove.
1 40 feet. Climb straight ahead on good holds. There is a short difficult section just before entering an open groove. Belay.
2 40 feet. Climb the slab on the right to a grassy ledge.

Ascend a little and again traverse right to a good platform with no satisfactory belay.

3 25 feet. The nose (crux) is best climbed from the left edge of the platform. Above it, a little groove is followed for a few feet, then a step right is taken. Finish straight ahead.

Deerstalker. 170 feet. Severe.
Starts 10 feet to the right of South Face Route, below an obvious groove slanting up to the right.

1 70 feet. Follow the groove for 20 feet until it is possible to make a difficult move into the upper groove which is followed to a poor stance. Use a piton for a belay.

2 100 feet. Step up to the right into the steep groove, which is climbed by jamming, to the first big foothold on the right wall. Step on to the left wall and climb straight up to the top on good holds.

Round How (219081)

This small glaciated crag on Great End lies just above the Corridor Route, a short distance from where the path crosses Greta Ghyll.

Wyvern Groove. 100 feet. Severe (mild).
An interesting little route on perfect rock. Runs up a deeply-cut groove near the right end of the crag.

1 30 feet. From the foot of the groove traverse the slab to the right until it is possible to traverse left back into the groove. Belay and poor stance. A very severe alternative to this pitch is to climb the groove direct by a series of short laybacks.

2 70 feet. Climb the groove, with difficulty, keeping to its right wall near the top. Easy rocks lead to the top.

ESK PIKE – The West Face (234077)

300 yards west of Esk Hause, and only slightly higher, is a cluster of short, stepped buttresses of excellent rock (similar to Esk Buttress). The main, central one gives three good pitches up the edge, above a gully on the right.

Esk Edge. 180 feet. Severe.

1 60 feet. From the foot of the gully, an obvious chimney-cave is ascended by bridging until it is possible to step out left on to a pedestal. The wall above, and some slabs, lead to belays below the second vertical wall.

2 60 feet. On the right edge of the wall is a block separated from the main mass by a deep crack. Gain the crack, and surmount the block with difficulty. Airy climbing up the wall above leads to easier ground and belays.

3 60 feet. Climb the grooved arête above.

LINGMELL (212084)

Pier's Ghyll. Severe (mild).

Best climbed on a hot day with a large jolly party. This is the extremely deep ravine on the eastern side of Lingmell, reached from Wasdale Head by following Lingmell Beck towards Sty Head and turning up around the low spur, which Lingmell sends down to the north.

The ghyll contains interesting scrambling but only three real pitches. After scrambling round and over various pools, a 20-foot pitch in front of a waterfall is climbed by bridging. This is only reached by wading through a deep pool.

More scrambling leads to a steep 20-foot corner with a difficult finish. Shortly after this, the ghyll widens and an escape may be made. The next pitch, which is again approached by wading tactics, is 40 feet high with a difficult start. More interesting scrambling leads to the Bridge Rock, which may be passed under, or to the right outside of the bridge.

The ghyll now turns to the left, leading past pools and small waterfalls and soon widens to finish near an outcrop of rock on the Corridor Route to Scafell.

Pilgrim's Progress. Very difficult.

An expedition of a similar nature to the previous route, which leads, in 2,000 feet of climbing and scrambling, to the top of Lingmell. The route follows Pier's Ghyll to just above the Bridge Rock where Straight Ghyll joins it from the right. The latter is then followed to Lingmell Crag which is climbed to the summit.

Ascend Pier's Ghyll to the first waterfall pitch and avoid it by climbing the left wall for 70 feet; then descend diagonally back to the bed of the ghyll. Continue to the Bridge Rock, avoiding the second waterfall pitch by climbing the right wall.

Above the Bridge Rock fork right and scramble up Straight Ghyll for some 500 feet, on poor rock, to a small cave below a chockstone; this is climbed on the left, for 70 feet. Good small holds will be found on the right wall.

Continue up the scoop above for 100 feet and climb the arête on the left for 200 feet to the summit.

Scafell Face

SCAFELL FACE		Grade	Page
HM	HIGH MAN	—	32
LM	LOW MAN	—	32
P	PISGAH	—	11
A	BROAD STAND	M	67
B	MICKLEDORE	—	9
C	NORTH OR PENRITH CLIMB	M	13
D	COLLIER'S CLIMB	S (hard)	13
E	KESWICK BROTHERS' CLIMB	VD	14
F	BOTTERILL'S SLAB	VS	15
G	CENTRAL BUTTRESS ..	VS (hard)	18
	G¹ THE OVAL	—	
	G² THE GREAT FLAKE ..	—	
H	MOSS GHYLL	VD (hard)	25
J	PISGAH BUTTRESS DIRECT ..	S (mild)	28
K	STEEP GHYLL	—	32
L	PINNACLE TERRACE	—	12
M	DEEP GHYLL	—	49
N	WEST WALL TRAVERSE ..	—	12
O	DEEP GHYLL BUTTRESS ..	—	49
O¹	UPPER DEEP GHYLL BUTTRESS	VS (mild)	49
R	TO CASTOR, POLLUX AND RED GHYLL BUTTRESS	—	54
S	SCAFELL SHAMROCK ..	—	56
XX	RAKE'S PROGRESS	—	12
YY	PATH BETWEEN LORD'S RAKE AND MICKLEDORE ..	—	12
ZZ	LORD'S RAKE	—	9

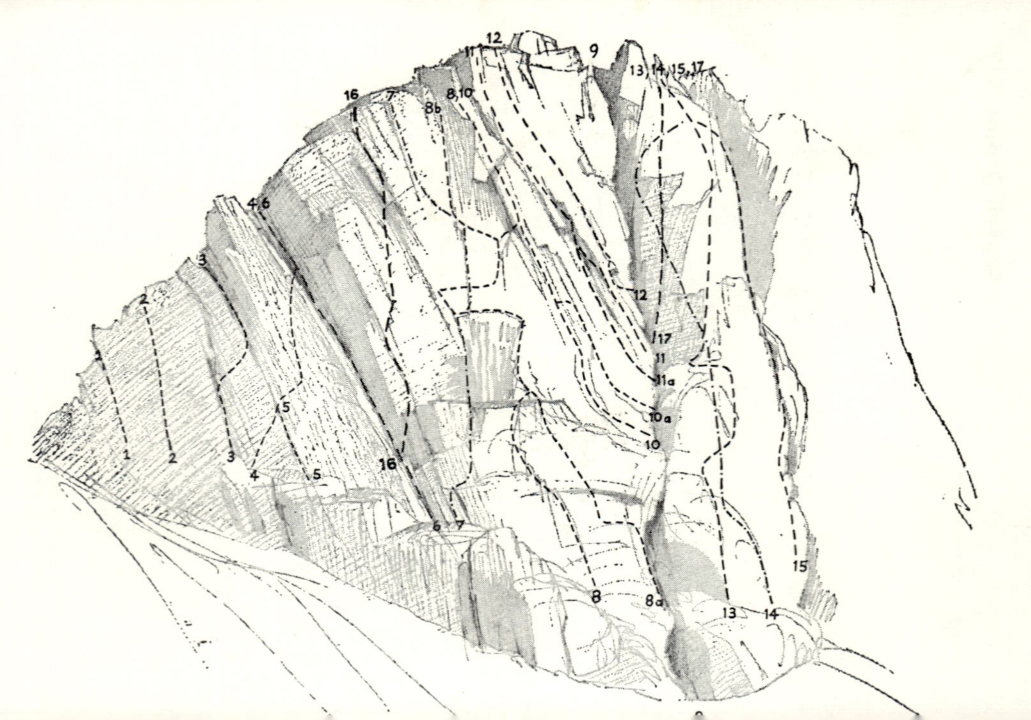

12
11
9
13 14 15,17
16
7
8,10
8b
4,6
3
2
12
17
11
11a
5
10a
10
1
2
3
16
4
5
6
7
15
8
8a
13
14

SCAFELL CRAG — CENTRAL BUTTRESS

		Grade	*Page*
1	NORTH OR PENRITH CLIMB	M	13
2	THE HANGING CHIMNEY ..	VS (hard)	13
3	COLLIER'S CLIMB	S (hard)	13
4	KESWICK BROTHERS' CLIMB	VD	14
5	TRICOUNI SLAB	S (mild)	15
6	BOTTERILL'S SLAB	VS	15
7	THE NAZGUL	XS	17
8	CENTRAL BUTTRESS ..	VS (hard)	18
	8a DIRECT START	VS (hard)	19
	8b DIRECT FINISH	VS (hard)	20
9	MOSS GHYLL	VD (hard)	25
10	MOSS GHYLL GROOVES ..	S (hard)	21
	10a VARIATION START ..	S (hard)	21
11	NARROW STAND	VS (hard)	23
11a	LAST STAND	XS	22
12	SLAB AND GROOVE	VS	23
13	PISGAH BUTTRESS DIRECT ..	S (mild)	28
14	MOSES TROD	S	30
15	BOS'N'S BUTTRESS	VS	30
16	THE WHITE WIZARD	XS	16
17	THE GRIPE	VS (hard)	28

L

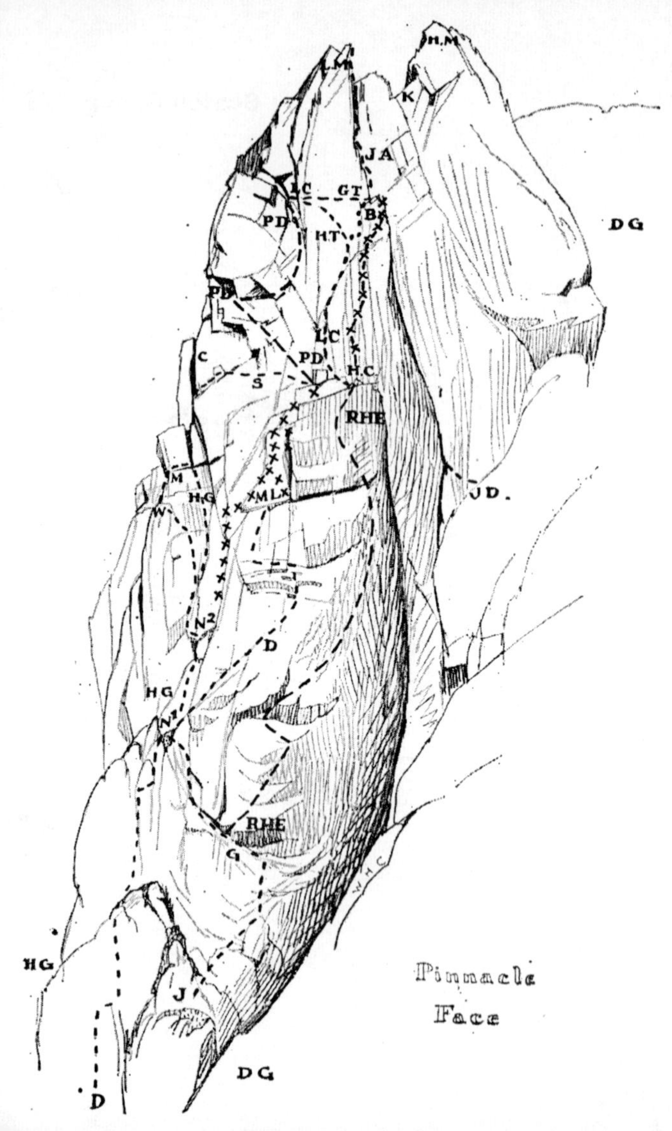

Pinnacle
Face

PINNACLE FACE

		Grade	Page
LM	LOW MAN	—	32
K	KNIFE-EDGE ARÊTE	—	32
HM	HIGH MAN	—	32
DG	DEEP GHYLL	—	49
HG	HOPKINSON'S GULLY ..	S (hard)	36
J	JONES'S ROUTE DIRECT FROM LORD'S RAKE	S	37
	G THE GANGWAY	—	
	N^1 FIRST NEST	—	
	N^2 SECOND NEST	—	
	W THE WAITING ROOM ..	—	
	M THE MANTELSHELF ..	—	
	C THE CREVASSE	—	
XX	DIRECT FROM LORD'S RAKE TO HOPKINSON'S CAIRN ..	S	38
	ML MOSS LEDGE	—	
HC	HOPKINSON'S CAIRN ..	—	
D	MOSS LEDGE DIRECT ..	VS (mild)	38
S	SANSOM'S TRAVERSE ..	—	47
RHE	RIGHT-HAND EDGE	VS (hard)	39
LC	LOW MAN FROM HOPKINSON'S CAIRN ..	D	39
X–X	JONES'S ARÊTE FROM HOPKINSON'S CAIRN ..	VS (mild)	40
	B THE BAD CORNER ..	—	
PD	PINNACLE FACE— DIRECT FINISH	VS (hard)	40
JD	JONES'S DIRECT FROM DEEP GHYLL	S (mild)	41
	JA JONES'S ARÊTE	—	41
	GT GIBSON'S TRAVERSE ..	—	42
	HT HOPKINSON AND TRIBE'S ROUTE	D (hard)	42

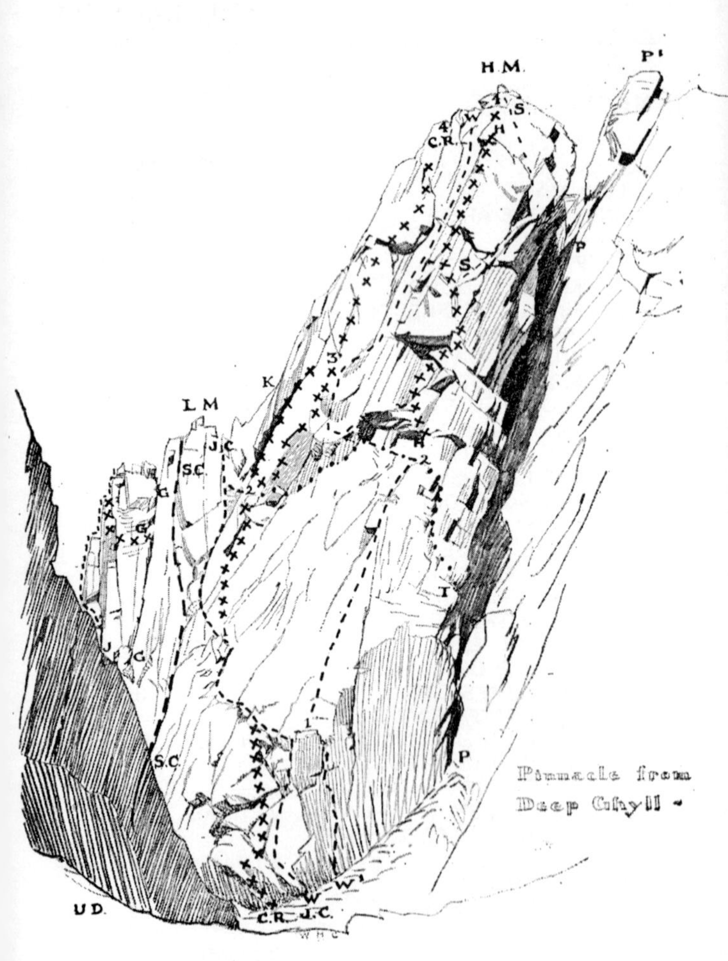

Pinnacle from Deep Ghyll -

PINNACLE FROM DEEP GHYLL

		Grade	Page
UD	UPPER DEEP GHYLL BUTTRESS	—	49
LM	LOW MAN	—	32
K	KNIFE-EDGE ARÊTE	—	32
P[1]	PISGAH	—	11
HM	HIGH MAN	—	32
J	JONES'S ROUTE FROM DEEP GHYLL	S (mild)	41
	G GIBSON'S CHIMNEY ..	S (mild)	42
	G[1] RECOMMENDED EXIT ..	—	42
SC	SLAB CLIMB	VS	42
CR	CENTRAL ROUTE— DEEP GHYLL SLABS ..	S (hard)	43
JC	JONES AND COLLIER'S CLIMB	VD	43
W	WOODHEAD'S CLIMB ..	S (mild)	44
	W[1] VARIATION START ..	—	
	H HERFORD'S FINISH ..	—	
	S de SELINCOURT'S FINISH	—	
P	PROFESSOR'S CHIMNEY ..	D	45
T	THOMPSON'S ROUTE ..	D	45

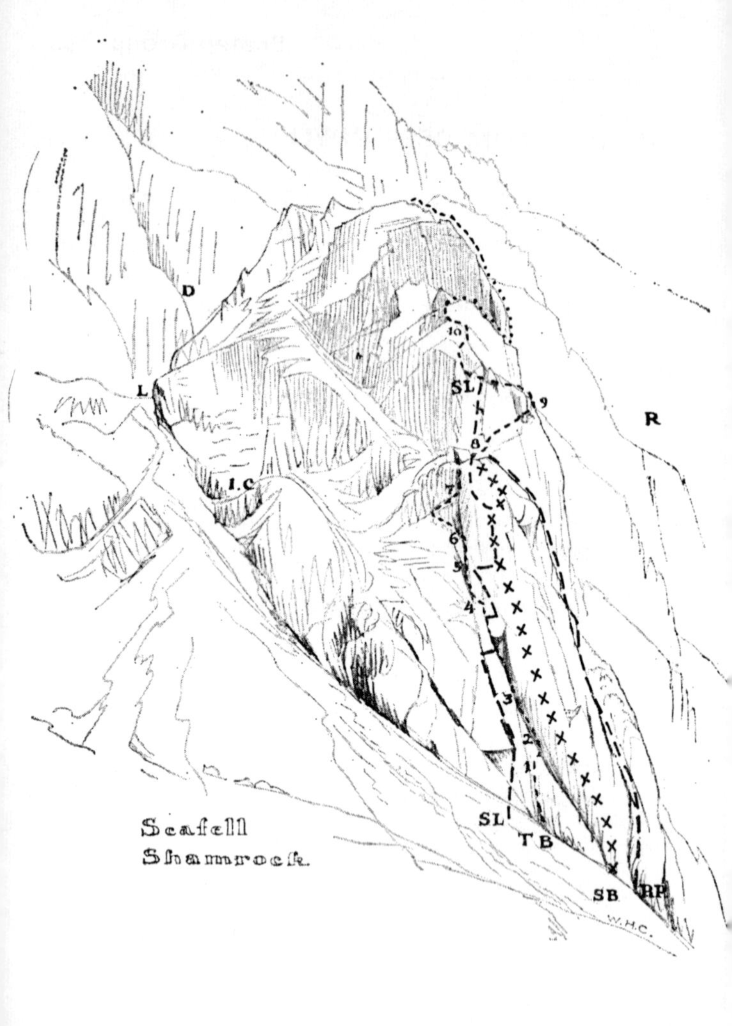
D
L
I.C
10
SL
9
R
8
7
6
5
4
3
2
1
SL
TB
SB
RP
W.H.C.
Scafell
Shamrock

SCAFELL SHAMROCK

		Grade	Page
L	LORD'S RAKE	—	11
D	DEEP GHYLL	—	49
IC	INTERMITTENT CHIMNEYS ..	M	56
SL	SILVER LINING	VS	57
TB	TOWER BUTTRESS	S (hard)	58
SB	SHAMROCK BUTTRESS ..	VS	59
RP	THE RAMPART	S (hard)	60
R	RED GHYLL	—	56

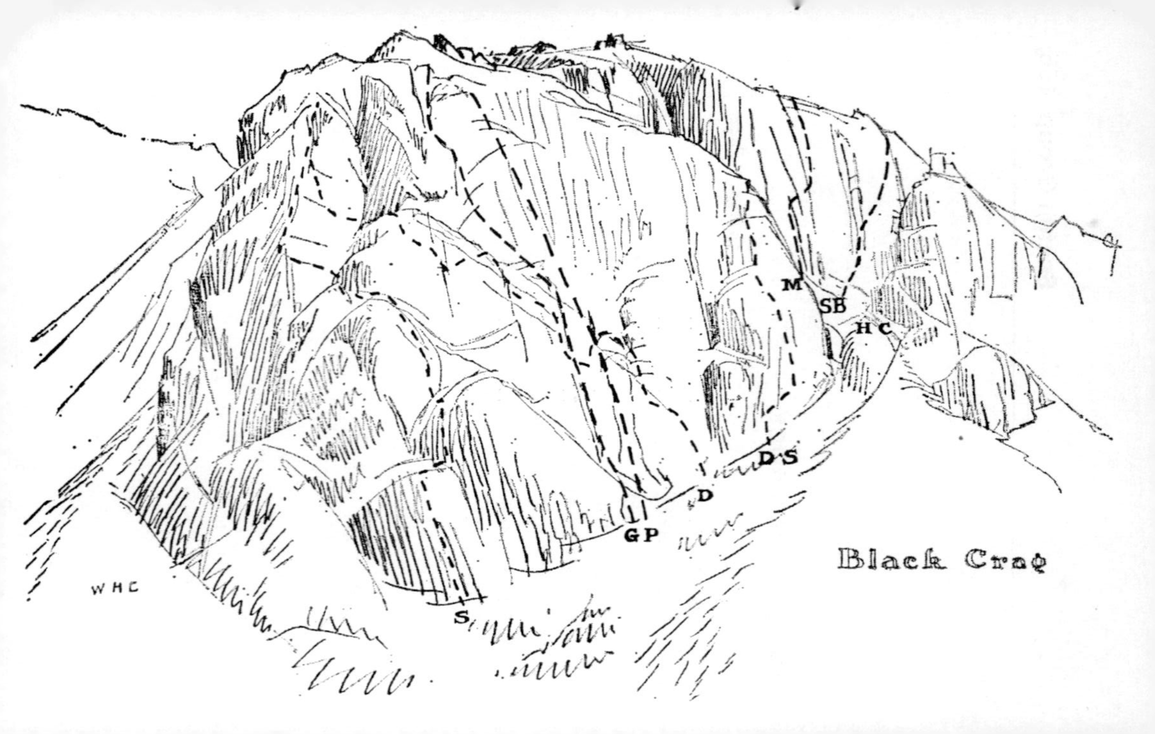

Black Crag

BLACK CRAG

		Grade	Page
S	SINISTER RIDGE	VD (hard)	61
G	GEODESIC	VS (hard)	63
P	PLUMB LINE	VS (mild)	63
D	THE DIAGONAL ROUTE ..	VS (mild)	64
DS	DEXTER SLAB	VD (hard)	65
M	MOUSETRAP	VS (hard)	66
SB	SHELOB	VS	66
HC	HOLE AND CORNER GULLY ..	M	66

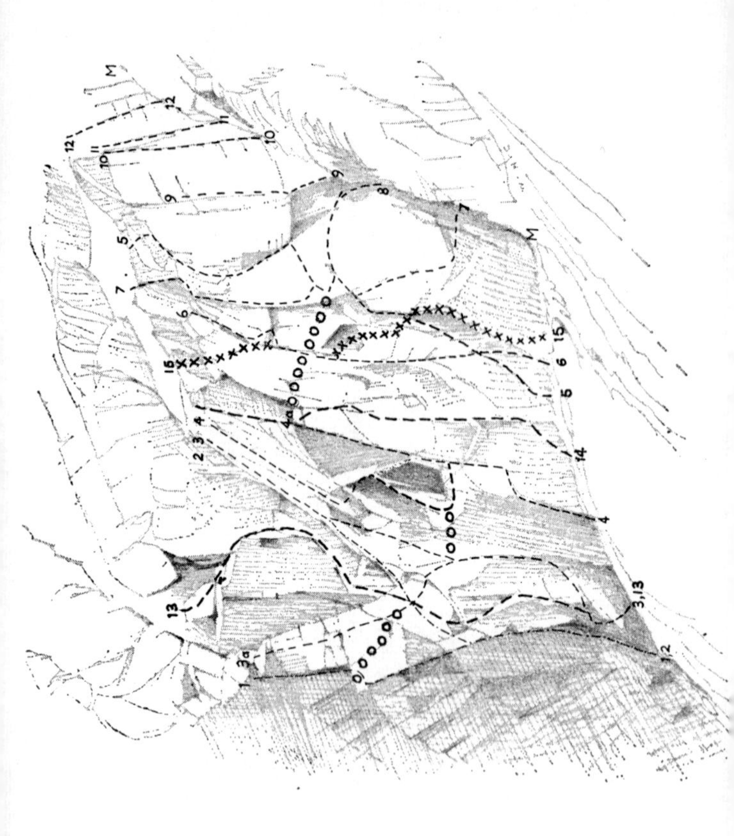

EAST BUTTRESS — RIGHT FLANK

		Grade	*Page*
1	ARMAGEDDON	VS (hard)	77
2	MOONDAY	VS (hard)	76
3	OVERHANGING WALL ..	VS	75
	3a WHITE SLAB VARIATION	—	75
4	MAY DAY CLIMB	VS (hard)	73
	4a DIRECT FINISH	VS (hard)	74
5	MICKLEDORE GROOVES ..	VS	71
6	LEVERAGE	XS	72
7	CHARTREUSE	VS (hard)	70
8	BARRY'S TRAVERSE	—	72
9	PERNOD	VS	68
10	TIA MARIA	VS	69
11	TIO PEPE	VS	69
12	ABSINTHE	VS (mild)	69
13	MINOTAUR	XS	76
14	DYAD	XS	73
15	THE FULCRUM	VS	71
000	THE LORD OF THE RINGS ..	XS	93
M	MICKLEDORE CHIMNEY ..	M	67

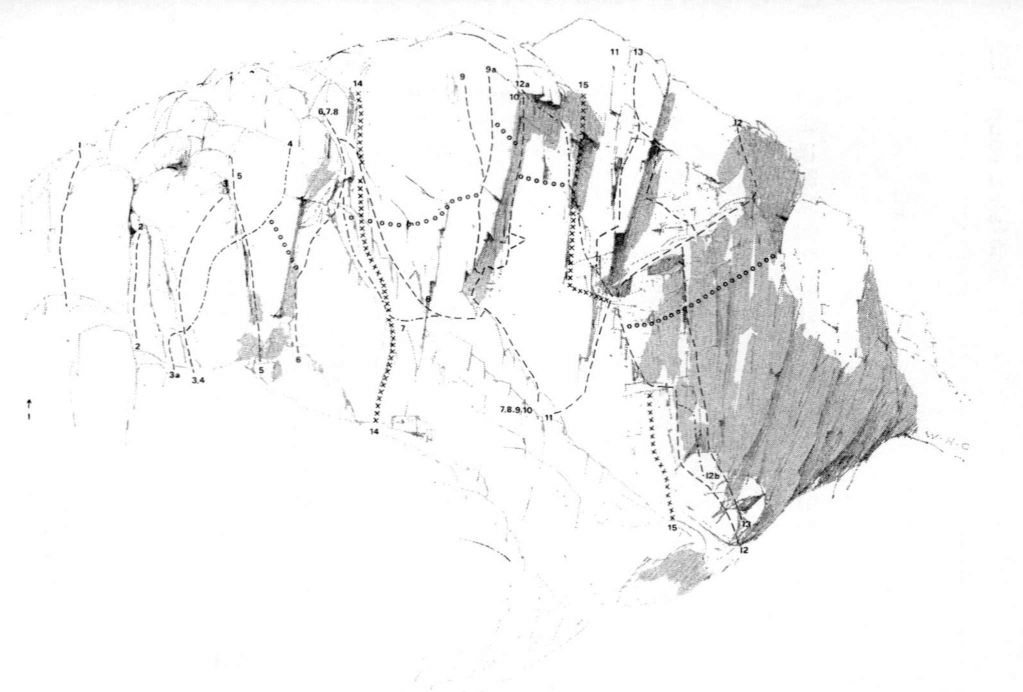
2
2
3a
3,4
4
5
5
6
6,7,8
7
8
9
9a
12a
10
14
14
15
15
11
11
13
13
12
12
12b
7,8,9,10
W.H.C.

EAST BUTTRESS — LEFT FLANK

		Grade	Page
1	SOUTH CHIMNEY	VS (hard)	90
2	SLIME CHIMNEY	VD	90
3	THE GREMLIN'S GROOVE	VS	89
	3a VARIATION START	—	90
4	HOLY GHOST	XS	89
5	TRINITY	VS (hard)	88
6	HELL'S GROOVE	VS (hard)	86
7	PEGASUS	VS (hard)	85
8	MORNING WALL	VS (mild)	84
9	PHOENIX	XS	83
	9a DIRECT FINISH	VS (hard)	84
10	ICHABOD	XS	82
11	THE OVERHANGING GROOVES	XS	82
12	GREAT EASTERN ROUTE	VS (mild)	79
	12a THE YELLOW SLAB	VS (hard)	80
	12b VARIATION START	VS (mild)	80
13	THE CENTAUR	VS (hard)	78
14	CHIMERA	VS (hard)	86
15	GOLD RUSH	XS	81
0000	THE LORD OF THE RINGS	XS	93

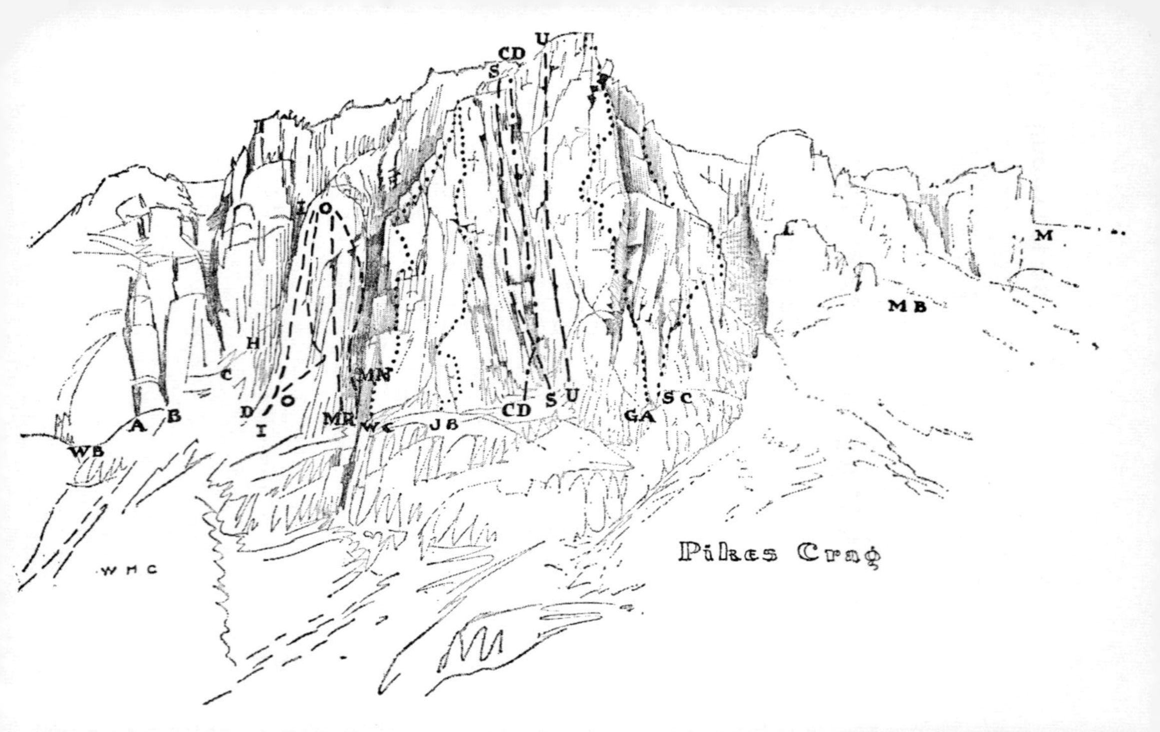
U
CD
S
I
O
H
C
D
O
I
MN
MR
WC
JB
CD
S
U
GA
SC
WB
A
B
MB
M
WHC
Pikes Crag

PIKE'S CRAG

		Grade	*Page*
M	MICKLEDORE	—	9
MB	MICKLEDORE BUTTRESS	—	102
SC	SOUTHERN CORNER	S	103
GA	GROOVED ARÊTE	VD	105
U	URCHIN'S GROOVE	S (hard)	107
S	THE SENTINEL	VS	108
CD	THE CITADEL	VS	108
JB	JUNIPER BUTTRESS	VD	109
WC	WALL AND CRACK	VD	110
MN	MARE'S NEST BUTTRESS	VS (mild)	111
MR	MARE'S RIB	VS	111
I	ISIS	VS (mild)	112
O	OSIRIS	VS	111
D	'D' GULLY	M	113
H	HORSE AND MAN ROCK	—	113
C	'C' GULLY	M	114
B	'B' GULLY	D (hard)	115
A	'A' GULLY	M	115
WB	WESTERN BUTTRESS	VD	115

GC
T
BR
CP
SR
RH
M
SC
B
BS
T
WP
S
R
CP
F
GS
BH
GG
GD
T
BS
R
BH
RH
SR
GG
WP
F
T
BR
M
B
GC
SC
GS
GD

ESK BUTTRESS

		Grade	Page
GG	GARGOYLE GROOVE ..	VS	117
GD	GARGOYLE DIRECT	VS	118
BH	BOOT HILL	VS (hard)	119
WP	WEST POINT	XS	120
GS	GARGOYLE'S STAIRS ..	S (hard)	119
F	FRUSTRATION	S (hard)	120
S	SATISFACTION	VS (hard)	121
R	RED EDGE	VS (hard)	122
BS	BLACK SUNDAY	VS (hard)	123
SC	SQUARE CHIMNEY ROUTE ..	VS	124
M	MEDUSA WALL	VS	125
B	BRIDGE'S ROUTE	S (hard)	126
CP	CENTRAL PILLAR	XS	127
GC	GREAT CENTRAL CLIMB ..	VS	128
T	TRESPASSER GROOVE ..	VS (hard)	129
BR	BOWER'S ROUTE	S (hard)	131
SR	SERPENT ROUTE	S (hard)	132
RH	RIGHT-HAND ROUTE ..	VS (hard)	133

EXTREMELY SEVERE

		Page
Central Pillar, The	Esk Buttress	127
Dyad	East Buttress	73
Gilt Edge Eliminate	Scafell Crag	56
Gold Rush	East Buttress	81
Grand Slam	Esk Buttress	118
Holy Ghost	East Buttress	89
Hydra	Esk Buttress	122
Ichabod	East Buttress	82
Incubus	East Buttress	87
Last Stand	Scafell Crag	22
Leverage	East Buttress	72
Lord of the Rings, The	East Buttress	93
Minotaur	East Buttress	76
Nazgul, The	Scafell Crag	17
Overhanging Grooves, The	East Buttress	82
Phoenix	East Buttress	83
West Point	Esk Buttress	120
White Wizard, The	Scafell Crag	16

VERY SEVERE (Hard)

Armageddon	East Buttress	77
Amoeba	Esk Buttress	122
Black Sunday	Esk Buttress	123
Blarney	Cam Spout Crag	100
Boot Hill	Esk Buttress	119
Cam Spout Buttress	Cam Spout Crag	96
Centaur, The	East Buttress	78
Central Buttress	Scafell Crag	18
Central Buttress by the Direct Start and Direct Finish	Scafell Crag	20
Central Buttress Girdle	Scafell Crag	24
Chartreuse	East Buttress	70
Chimera	East Buttress	86
Clockwork Orange	Scafell Crag	28
East Buttress Girdle	East Buttress	91
Edge Hog	Scafell Crag	41

VERY SEVERE (Hard) (cont'd).		Page
Eskdale Grooves	Cam Spout Crag	97
Existentialism	Cam Spout Crag	101
Geodesic	Black Crag	63
Great Eastern by the Yellow Slab Variation	East Buttress	80
Gripe, The	Scafell Crag	28
Hanging Chimney, The	Scafell Crag	13
Hell's Groove	East Buttress	86
Manhanger	Cam Spout Crag	97
May Day Climb	East Buttress	73
May Day—Direct Finish	East Buttress	74
Moonday	East Buttress	76
Mousetrap, The	Black Crag	66
Narrow Stand	Scafell Crag	23
Orc, The	Cam Spout Crag	100
Pegasus	East Buttress	85
Pinnacle Face—Direct Finish	Scafell Crag	40
Pisgah Ya Bas	Scafell Crag	31
Red Edge, The	Esk Buttress	122
Right-hand Edge	Scafell Crag	39
Right-hand Route	Esk Buttress	133
Satisfaction	Esk Buttress	121
South Chimney	East Buttress	90
Trespasser Groove	Esk Buttress	129
Trinity	East Buttress	88
Vargtime	Cam Spout Crag	96
Xerxes	Scafell Crag	53

VERY SEVERE

Banner's Exit to Moss Ghyll	Scafell Crag	27
Bos'n's Buttress	Scafell Crag	30
Botterill's Slab	Scafell Crag	15
Cam Spout Grooves	Cam Spout Crag	98
Citadel, The	Pike's Crag	108
Ent, The	Cam Spout Crag	99
Fulcrum, The	East Buttress	71

VERY SEVERE (Mild) (cont'd).		Page
Morning Wall	East Buttress	84
Moss	Esk Buttress	117
Moss Ledge Direct	Scafell Crag	38
Plumb Line	Black Crag	63
Steep Ghyll Grooves	Scafell Crag	31
Upper Deep Ghyll Buttress	Scafell Crag	49
Waiting Room from 1st Pitch Steep Ghyll	Scafell Crag	34
SEVERE (Hard)		
Bower's Route	Esk Buttress	131
Bridge's Route	Esk Buttress	126
Central Route—Deep Ghyll Slabs	Scafell Crag	43
Collier's Climb	Scafell Crag	13
Frustration	Esk Buttress	120
Gargoyle's Stairs	Esk Buttress	119
Girdle Traverse	Scafell Crag	46
Hopkinson's Gully	Scafell Crag	36
Jacob's Ladder	Scafell Crag	51
Moss Ghyll Grooves	Scafell Crag	21
Pinnacle Face from Steep Ghyll	Scafell Crag	35
Rampart, The	Scafell Crag	60
Serpent Route	Esk Buttress	132
Slanting Groove	Pike's Crag	105
Tower Buttress, The	Scafell Crag	58
Urchin's Groove	Pike's Crag	107
SEVERE		
Afterthought	Esk Buttress	117
Deerstalker	Stand Crag,	142
Direct from Lord's Rake to Hopkinson's Cairn	Scafell Crag	38
Esk Edge	Esk Pike	143
Jones's Route Direct from Lord's Rake	Scafell Crag	37

SEVERE (cont'd).		Page
Moses' Trod	Scafell Crag	30
Narrowcove Buttress	Rough Crag	138
Slabs Direct—Grooved Arête	Pike's Crag	
South Face Route	Stand Crag	141
Southern Corner	Pike's Crag	103
Wall Finish	Esk Buttress	136
SEVERE (Mild)		
All Sorts	Stand Crag	141
Jones's Route from Deep Ghyll	Scafell Crag	41
Keswick Brothers' Climb (Variation Finish)	Scafell Crag	14
Low Man by Right Wall of Steep Ghyll	Scafell Crag	32
Pier's Ghyll	Lingmell	143
Pisgah Buttress Direct	Scafell Crag	28
Red Ghyll Wall	Scafell Crag	55
Sector	Pike's Crag	104
Steeplechase	Pike's Crag	114
Thor's Cave	Esk Buttress	137
Tricouni Slab	Scafell Crag	15
Upper West Wall Climb	Scafell Crag	50
Woodhead's Climb	Scafell Crag	44
Wyvern Groove	Round How	142
VERY DIFFICULT (Hard)		
Dexter Slab	Black Crag	65
Moss Ghyll	Scafell Crag	25
Pollux	Scafell Crag	54
Sinister Ridge	Black Crag	61
VERY DIFFICULT		
Brother's Crack	Great End	139
Chimney Buttress	Esk Buttress	136

VERY DIFFICULT (cont'd).

Eros	Stand Crag	141
Great Chimney	Scafell Crag	51
Grooved Arête	Pike's Crag	105
Jones and Collier's Climb	Scafell Crag	43
Juniper Buttress	Pike's Crag	109
Keswick Brothers' Climb	Scafell Crag	14
Pike's Crag Ridge	Pike's Crag	112
Pilgrim's Progress	Lingmell	144
Pisgah Buttress (Original Route)	Scafell Crag	29
Red Ghyll Buttress	Scafell Crag	56
Slime Chimney	East Buttress	90
Thunder Rib	Esk Buttress	137
Wall and Crack Climb	Pike's Crag	110
Western Buttress	Pike's Crag	115

DIFFICULT (Hard)

'B' Gully	Pike's Crag	115
High Man via Slingsby's Chimney	Scafell Crag	33

DIFFICULT

Collier's Climb (Variation Start)	Scafell Crag	13
Cremation Ridge	Pike's Crag	103
Low Man from Hopkinson's Cairn	Scafell Crag	39
Little Buttress	Stand Crag	140
Mickledore Buttress No. 1	Pike's Crag	102
Mickledore Buttress, Western Corner	Pike's Crag	102
Mickledore Chimney, Direct Finish	Scafell Crag	67
Pisgah from Jordan Gap	Scafell Crag	46
Professors Chimney	Scafell Crag	45

List of First Ascents

Broad Stand. Probably early in the nineteenth century. Mentioned in Green's Guide. S. G. Collingwood suggests that Coleridge may have ascended it.

1869	North or Penrith Climb	Major Ponsonby R. E. Cundill
1869	Mickledore Chimney (Easy Finish) 12 Sept. 1893. Direct finish Petty's Rift	C. W. Dymond W. H. Fowler W. P. Haskett-Smith
1882	April. Deep Ghyll (Descent in deep snow) Aug.-Sept. 1882. W. P. Haskett-Smith	A. L. Mumm J. E. King
1882	Aug.-Sept. Central Gully, Great End	W. P. Haskett-Smith
1882	Aug.-Sept. South-east Gully, Great End	W. P. Haskett-Smith
1884	Sept. 3. Scafell Pinnacle, High Man from Jordan Gap	W. P. Haskett-Smith
1884	Sept. 20. Steep Ghyll, Low Man, High Man	W. P. Haskett-Smith J. W. Robinson
1888	July 15. High Man via Steep Ghyll and Slingsby's Chimney	W. Cecil Slingsby Geoffrey Hastings E. Hopkinson W. P. Haskett-Smith

June 1912. Variation to the left of the chimney. G. S. Sansom.

1892	Dec. 26. Moss Ghyll, Collie Exit	J. N. Collie G. Hastings J. W. Robinson

The crux was mastered by chipping a foothold in the rock with an ice axe; the first recorded use of an artificial aid in rock-climbing.

1893	April 2. Hopkinson and Tribe's Route	C. Hopkinson W. N. Tribe
1893	April 2. Collier's Climb	J. Collier S. B. Winser
1893	Easter Monday. Brigg's Climb, Great End	J. T. Brigg W. A. Brigg Alfred Homes
	Aug. 1884. Descended by a large party including, C. N. Williamson, Bryden, Zperro, three ladies, and W. P. Haskett-Smith.	
1893	April 29. Pier's Ghyll	J. Collier S. B. Winser H. S. W. Jones G. Fairbairn
1894	Sept. 9. 'A' Gully, Pike's Crag	W. H. Fowler H. W. Blunt
1894	Sept. 16. 'B' Gully, Pike's Crag	W. H. Fowler H. W. Blunt
	N.B.—One of these gullies was climbed by W. P. Haskett-Smith in 1882, and another in 1844 (probably as it was repeated) with O. G. Jones on his first visit to the district.	
1895	Sept. 23. Great Chimney	V. Blake A. W. Southall
1896	April 20. Jones's Route from Deep Ghyll	O. G. Jones A. P. Abraham G. D. Abraham
	1904. Gibson's Chimney. A. H. Binns.	
1897	July 12. Keswick Brother's Climb	G. D. Abraham A. P. Abraham J. W. Puttrell
	25 Dec. 1897. Variation Finish. O. G. Jones.	
1898	April 19. Jones's Route Direct from Lord's Rake	O. G. Jones G. T. Walker
	An important breakaway from gully and chimney climbing; executed in stockinged feet.	

1898	April 22. Jones and Colliers' Climb	O. G. Jones
1898	April 22. Pisgah Buttress	O. G. Jones G. D. Abraham A. P. Abraham

1 Sept. 1910. From Tennis Court Ledge to the Fives Court, omitting crack. N. C. Maden, H. R. Pope.
6 July 1911. Direct Route. S. W. Herford, F. M. J. McConechy.

1898	Sept. 10. West Wall Climb	J. W. Robinson T. H. Doncaster H. W. Blunt
1900	June 1. Thompson's Route, Scafell Pinnacle	P. S. Thompson P. A. Thompson
1903	June 2. Botterill's Slab	F. Botterill H. Williamson J. E. Grant

Climbed in nailed boots with rucksack and ice-axe!

1903	April 12. Peregrine Gully	P. Lund C. Becker T. Gray
1907	Aug. 24. Woodhead's Climb	A. G. Woodhead W. L. Collinson

10 July 1913. Herford's Direct Finish. S. W. Herford, S. F. Jeffcoat.

1910	Aug. 24. Brothers' Crack	G. F. Woodhouse A. J. Woodhouse
1911	Sept. Upper West Wall Climb	J. Laycock H. B. Gibson S. W. Herford
1912	April 17. Direct from Lord's Rake to Hopkinson's Cairn	S. W. Herford G. S. Sansom

1912 June 19. Hopkinson's Gully — S. W. Herford, G. S. Sansom

30 Dec. 1887. The lower portion of this climb was ascended and descended, under icy conditions by C. Hopkinson and two of the following, H. W. Holder, H. J. Wooley, E. W. Bury. While not a first ascent, the history of Scafell Pinnacle would be incomplete without this record.

1912 Sept. 14. Girdle Traverse of Scafell — S. W. Herford, G. S. Sansom, W. B. Brunskill, H. B. Gibson

7 June 1919. Ascent of Bad Corner. H. M. Kelly, G. S. Bower, Mrs. Kelly, R. E. W. Pritchard.
30 July 1919. Jones's Arête from Hopkinson's Cairn. C. G. Crawford, H. M. Kelly, C. F. Holland.
5 Aug. 1923. Traverse from Fives Court to Botterill's Exit from Moss Ghyll. H. B. Lyon, T. R. Burnett, M. Mabel Barker, H. P. Cain.

1913 May 13. Wayfarer's Crack, Great End — S. W. Herford, J. Laycock

1914 April 20 and 22. Central Buttress — S. W. Herford, G. S. Sansom

Probably the biggest single breakthrough in standard in the history of Lakeland climbing. H. B. Gibson and D. G. Murray were in the party on the first day when the Flake Crack was climbed.
On the first ascent, a rope cradle was arranged at the chockstone of the Flake Crack. In this, the second man sat and from his shoulders the leader was able to reach the top of the Flake.
Aug. 1931. Flake crack, without assistance at the chockstone. J. M. Edwards, W. W. Stallybrass, M. Pallis.
6 Oct. 1932. Bayonet-shaped crack. M. Linnell.
June 1934. Direct Finish. F. G. Balcombe, J. Wright, J. R. Files.
26 July 1939. Variation Start. A. Mullan, H. Thompson.

1919 July 28. Low Man by the Right Wall of Steep Ghyll — C. F. Holland, H. M. Kelly, C. G. Crawford

1919 July 30. Waiting Room from First Pitch in Steep Ghyll — C. G. Crawford, H. M. Kelly

1919 Aug. 5. Pinnacle Face from First Pitch in Steep Ghyll — C. R. Crawford, C. F. Holland

1920	May 16. Bower's Climb, Esk Buttress	G. S. Bower A. W. Wakefield P. R. Masson

Frankland's Finish. C. D. Frankland, B. Beetham.
11 June 1929. Kirkus's Variation. C. F. Kirkus, A. B. Hargreaves.

1920	May 23. Upper Deep Ghyll Buttress	H. M. Kelly R. E. W. Pritchard G. S. Bower

8 June 1946. Variation pitch 4. A. R. Dolphin, J. W. Cook.

1920	Aug. 29. Central Route, Deep Ghyll Slabs	H. M. Kelly G. S. Bower R. E. W. Pritchard
1921	Sept. 9. Little Buttress, Stand Crag	F. Graham
1921	Sept. 9. Rowan Tree Buttress, Stand Crag	C. F. Holland Miss Rathbone
1922	Sept. 10. Red Ghyll Buttress	W. Eden-Smith H. M. Kelly
1923	Mar. 22. Esk Chimneys	W. T. Elmslie N. M. P. Reilly H. Mackintosh
1923	Easter. Cam Spout Buttress	C. D. Frankland W. V. Brown G. Addyman

This route is not recorded in the text as three generations of guide-books writers have been unable to locate it. (This route is not to be confused with Cam Spout Buttress climbed by J. A. Austin and N. J. Soper in 1964.)

1924	April 21. Wall and Crack Climb, Pike's Crag	H. M. Kelly R. E. W. Pritchard Blanche Eden-Smith Graham Wilson

N.B.—The lower portion of the climb was done by C. F. Holland a day or two earlier.

1924	April 22. Juniper Buttress, Pike's Crag	H. M. Kelly R. E. W. Pritchard N. L. Eden-Smith W. Eden-Smith
1924	April 23. Grooved Arête, Pike's Crag 1 March 1934. Slabs direct. G. Barratt, T. A. Medleycot.	C. F. Holland G. R. Speaker
1924	April 23. Southern Corner, Pike's Crag	H. M. Kelly Blanche Eden-Smith N. L. Eden-Smith W. Eden-Smith
1924	Sept. 27. Western Buttress, Pike's Crag 21 Sept. 1949. Pitches 4 and 5. E.S.W., S.A.	F. Graham
1925	April 14. Castor	H. M. Kelly R. E. W. Pritchard
1925	April 14. Pollux	H. M. Kelly R. E. W. Pritchard
1925	June 5. Slime Chimney	C. D. Frankland B. Beetham A. W. Wakefield J. Wright
1925	June 18. The Banister	Blanche Eden-Smith H. M. Kelly
1925	June 22. Sinister Ridge, Black Crag	H. M. Kelly Blanche Eden-Smith
1925	June 22. Hole and Corner Gully, Black Crag	H. M. Kelly Blanche Eden-Smith
1925	Aug. 25. Dexter Slab, Black Crag	H. M. Kelly Blanche Eden-Smith R. E. W. Pritchard

1925 Aug. 30. South Face Route, Stand Crag — F. Graham, C. B. Jerram

1925 Sept. 3. Intermittent Chimneys, Scafell Shamrock — R. E. W. Pritchard, H. M. Kelly, Blanche Eden-Smith

1925 Sept. 3. Tower Buttress, Scafell Shamrock — H. M. Kelly, R. E. W. Pritchard, Blanche Eden-Smith

Direct Finish. P. Hogg.

1925 Sept. 6. Moss Ledge Direct, Scafell Pinnacle — F. Graham, G. M. Wellburn

1926 July 1. Moss Ghyll Grooves — H. M. Kelly, Blanche Eden-Smith, J. B. Kilshaw

A classic climb by one of the leading pioneers of the time.
July 1946. Variation Start. T. G. Peirson, M. H. McFarlane.

1927 Aug. 5. Mickledore Buttress, Western Corner — G. Wood-Johnson, E. F. Whiteley

1928 Aug. 6. Diagonal Route, Black Crag — F. Graham, G. M. Wellburn

1 April 1960. Direct Finish. J. A. Austin, J. M. Austin.

1931 May. Mickledore Grooves — C. F. Kirkus, I. M. Waller, M. Pallis

A bold lead, opening up a new phase in Scafell's history.
20 Sept. 1936. The Slab Start. R. V. M. Barry, C. G. T. Collin.
24 May 1959. Direct Finish, D. W. English, D. Beattie, M. V. McKenzie.

1932 July 10. Bridge's Climb, Esk Buttress — A. W. Bridge, A. B. Hargreaves, M. Linnell, W. S. Dyson

1932 Aug. 21. Great Eastern Route — M. Linnell, S. H. Cross

10 Sept. 1933. Yellow Slab Variation. M. Linnell, H. Pearson. The Yellow Slab finish was one of the most serious leads of the period.
2 Aug. 1937. Variation Start. H. Pearson, L. Kiernan.

1933 July 23. Overhanging Wall — M. Linnell, A. T. Hargreaves

10 Sept. 1932. White Slab Variation. M. Linnell, H. Pearson.

1933 Aug. 13. Morning Wall — A. T. Hargreaves, W. Clegg, M. Linnell

1936 June 20. Jacob's Ladder — A. T. Hargreaves, S. H. Cross

1936 June 21. Grey Bastion — S. H. Cross, A. T. Hargreaves, R. E. Hargreaves

1937 Oct. 2. Sector, Pike's Crag — A. T. Hargreaves, E. C. Spence, R. E. Hargreaves

1938 April 16. The Rampart — S. H. Cross, H. M. Kelly, A. M. Nelson, C. J. Astley Cooper

On the first ascent the groove on pitch 5 was avoided. The firs complete ascent was made on 14 Aug. 1938, by S. H. Cross, A. T. Hargreaves, and C.S.S.

1938 May 1. May Day Climb — R. J. Birkett, C. W. Hudson, C. R. Wilson

The first contribution by an outstanding climber who was to play a large part in the exploration of the area.
21 June 1959. Direct Finish. G. Oliver, L. Willis.

1938	Aug. 7. East Buttress Girdle	R. J. Birkett L. Muscroft

N.B.—A. T. and R. E. Hargreaves, A. M. Cross and S. H. Cross did the second ascent 5 June 1940 but, through ignorance of the original route, took a different line between Mickledore Grooves and Overhanging Wall. Some of it proved to be more natural and consistent than the original so the guide writers took the liberty of combining the best pitches of both routes to form the one excellent traverse described. (R. Miller, 1956.)

1938	Sept. 18. Tricouni Slab	A. Mullan L. Mack
1939	May 13. Urchin's Groove	S. H. Cross A. M. Nelson
1939	May 29. The Citadel	S. H. Cross A. T. Hargreaves R. E. Hargreaves A. M. Nelson
1939	Aug. Plumb Line, Black Crag	S. H. Cross A. M. Nelson
1940	April 22. Pilgrim's Progress	B. Beetham
1941	June 22. Red Ghyll Wall	A. T. Hargreaves S. H. Cross R. E. Hargreaves A. M. Cross
1941	Aug. 21. Pike's Crag Ridge	B. Beetham J. B. Meldrum
1943	April 4. Wriggling Route	W. Peascod L. Kellett
1944	July 23. Girdle Traverse, Esk Buttress	R. J. Birkett T. Hill G. Dwyer

17 June 1956. Variations. W. Dowlen, J. Smith.

1944	Aug. 13. Serpent Route	R. J. Birkett T. Hill

1944	Sept. 10 Afterthought	R. J. Birkett T. Hill
1944	Sept. 10. Frustration	R. J. Birkett T. Hill
	Direct Finish. Satisfaction, P. Ross, F. Carroll, 30 May 1959.	
1944	Sept. 17. Chimney Buttress	R. J. Birkett T. Hill
1945	July 8. Great Central Climb	R. J. Birkett T. Hill
1945	July 28. Steep Ghyll Grooves	R. J. Birkett T. Hill
1945	July 29. Gremlin's Groove	R. J. Birkett T. Hill L. Muscroft
	2 Aug. 1963. Variation Start. L. J. Griffin, J. Wilkinson.	
1945	Aug. 12. South Chimney	R. J. Birkett T. Hill
	T. Hill led the last pitch.	
1945	Oct. 7. Gargoyle's Stairs	R. J. Birkett T. Hill
1945	Oct. 14. Thor's Cave	T. Hill R. J. Birkett
1945	Oct. 14. Thunder Rib	R. J. Birkett T. Hill
1947	Aug. 9. Medusa Wall	A. R. Dolphin L. J. Griffin
1947	Aug. 9. Gargoyle Groove	A. R. Dolphin L. J. Griffin
1947	Aug. 17. Square Chimney Route	R. J. Birkett L. Muscroft

1948	Aug. 28. Slab and Groove	R. J. Birkett L. Muscroft
	A fine culmination to Birkett's activities on Scafell.	
1952	May 17. Pegasus	A. R. Dolphin P. Greenwood
1952	May 24. Hell's Groove	A. R. Dolphin P. Greenwood
	P. Greenwood led the overhanging crack. Another significant step in climbing standards. Aug. 28 1972. Direct Finish. J. Adams and C. Read. (alt. leads).	
1952	Sept. 6. Trespasser Groove	A. R. Dolphin D. Hopkins
1952	Sept. 14. Mare's Nest Buttress, Pike's Crag	D. C. Birch J. Lovell
1953	April. All Sorts, Stand Crag	J. R. Wilkinson A. Beanland J. D. J. Wildridge
1954	April 16. Central Scoop, Round How	J. D. J. Wildridge R. Scott E. Barlow
	This route is not recorded in the text as the guide book writers were unable to locate it.	
1954	May 9. Wyvern Groove, Round Howe	J. R. Wilkinson H. Williamson J. A. Wood
1954	June 5. Tia Maria	H. Drasdo K. Finlay
1955	April 21. Eros	P. Ross R. Scott D. Wildridge
1955	April 21. Deerstalker	P. Ross R. Scott D. Wildridge

1955	June 5. Trinity	D. D. Whillans J. Sutherland
1957	May 2. Tio Pepe	G. J. Sutton E. G. D. Roberts
1957	Aug. 1. Phoenix	R. Moseley

Although not generally realized at the time this climb was a full grade harder than anything else on the crag.
Variation finish added 18 June 1967 by A. G. Cram and W. Young.

1958	May 3. Chartreuse	R. Smith D. Leaver
1958	May 3. Leverage	R. Smith D. Leaver

A superb day's work by one of Britain's best climbers.

1959	April 4. Pernod	G. Oliver F. Carrol

Sept. 1971. Direct Finish. P. Braithwaite, D. Little.

1959	Aug. 21. Bos'n's Buttress	H. I. Banner L. J. Griffin
1959	Aug. 22. Narrow Stand	H. I. Banner J. P. O'Neill L. J. Griffin
1959	Aug. 30. Xerxes	L. Brown C. E. M. Yates
1959	Sept. 13. Moonday	L. Brown J. Gerrard

12 Sept. 1971. Doomwatch Finish. A. D. Barley, A. Roche using 3 points of aid. Climbed free by J. Adams and C. Read 28 Aug. 1972.

1960	April 21. Armageddon	L. Brown G. Lund
1960	May 28. Ichabod	G. Oliver G. Arkless G. Arkless L. Willis

An additional piton was used on pitch 2.

1960	Easter. The Sentinel	P. Fearnehaugh J. Wright
1960	Whit. The Left Edge	L. O. Kendall D. W. English
1960	Whit. Right-hand Edge	J. J. S. Allison C. J. F. Rowbotham
1960	June 30. The Centaur	L. Brown S. Read

A fine route, culminating Brown's exploration of the East Buttress.

1961	May 14. Cremation Ridge	E. Ivison D. R. Greenop
1961	May 21. Direct Finish, Pinnacle Face	C. J. F. Rowbotham J. J. S. Allison
1962	Mar. 24. Right-hand Route	J. A. Austin E. Metcalf

20 June 1964. Direct Finish. J. A. Austin, D. Miller, D. G. Roberts.
Easter 1962. Flake Climb, J. A. Austin, D. W. Austin, E. Metcalf.

1962	Easter. Wall Finish	J. A. Austin D. W. Austin E. Metcalf
1962	June 3. Gargoyle Direct	D. W. English M. McKenzie K. Brannon
1962	June 17. Central Pillar	P. Crew M. Owen
1962	June 17. Black Sunday	J. A. Austin E. Metcalf N. J. Soper

1962	June 17. The Red Edge	J. A. Austin N. J. Soper E. Metcalf

A day of frenzied activity on Esk Buttress as, in the true traditions of a non-competitive sport, two rival parties raced for the Central Pillar, the last of the Lakeland 'plums'. Crew's party won, after a dawn start, while the others found first class 'consolation prizes.

1962	The Slab Climb	J. J. S. Allison R. J. Mansfield
1963	June 1. The Hanging Chimney	J. J. S. Allison R. J. Mansfield
1963	June 3. Steeplechase	D. N. Greenop E. Ivison
1963	June. The Overhanging Grooves	J. J. S. Allison C. H. Mitchell D. Moy
1963	July. Moses Trod	L. J. Griffin J. Wilkinson
1963	July. Absinthe	L. J. Griffin J. Wilkinson
1963	July. Mare's Rib	L. J. Griffin J. Wilkinson
1963	Aug. 1. Shamrock Buttress	L. J. Griffin J. Wilkinson
1963	Sept. 15. Cam Spout Grooves	J. A. Austin N. J. Soper
1964	Whit. Cam Spout Buttress	J. A. Austin N. J. Soper
1965	April. Holy Ghost	C. J. S. Bonington M. Thompson

A similar, but higher line was done by R. Moseley in 1957.

1966	June 2. Shelob	K. I. Meldrum W. Blake

1966	June 12. Silver Lining	D. W. English J. Wilkinson R. Valentine L. J. Griffin
1966	July 22. The Nazgul	L. Brown K. Jackson

One of the 'last great problems', climbed in typical Brown secrecy. Inquisitive competitors were told he was exploring Far East Buzzard Crag.

1966	The Ent.	M. A. Toole S. J. Brannan
1966	Oct. 29. The Orc	M. A. Toole B. Henderson
1966	Oct. 30. Esk Edge	J. R. Sutcliffe D. Chapman
1967	March 18. Blarney	M. A. Toole J. Rafferty Alternate Leads
1967	Hydra	R. J. Isherwood C. H. Taylor

Aid reduced to 1 piton by J. A. Austin.

1968	June. Dyad	K. Jackson C. Read Alternate Leads
1968	June 1. Gobsite	T. Martin J. Wilson Alternate Leads
1968	June 4. Slanting Groove	G. Milburn D. Gregory Alternate Leads
1968	June 16. The Fulcrum	K. Jackson J. Adams Alternate Leads

1968	June 16. Saxifrage Ridge, Black Crag	K. I. Meldrum J. R. Lees Alternate Leads
1968	June 16. The Mousetrap, Black Crag	K. I. Meldrum J. R. Lees Alternate Leads
1968	June 16. Minotaur	S. Clarke G. Oliver H. Loughran G. Lowes Varied Leads
1968	July 6. Narrow Cove Buttress 6.7.68 Direct Finish J. R. Sutcliffe, P. Allerton	D. Chapman P. W. Green
1968	Aug. 11. Long Stand	E. N. Cross N. J. Soper G. Dyke G. Valentine Alternate Leads
1968	Aug. 21. Isis	I. Roper J. Wilkinson
1968	Aug. 21. Osiris	I. Roper J. Wilkinson
1969	April 20. Eskdale Grooves	M. Goff J. Dawson
1969	May 17. Boot Hill	W. Young A. G. Cram Alternate Leads
1969	June 7. Chimera	W. Young A. G. Cram Varied Leads
1969	June 14th. Gold Rush	A. G. Cram W. Young

1969	June 14/15. The Lord of the Rings	J. Adams C. Read Alternate Leads
1969	Aug. 16. Gilt Edge Eliminate	C. Read R. Lake Alternate Leads
	A magnificent achievement taking an eliminate line across the buttress. A last great problem solved.	
1969	Aug. 31. The Spout	D. Musgrove D. D. Gray R. J. Cummaford Alternate Leads
1969	Sept. 30. Vargtime	M. Goff J. Duff
	The point of aid was dispensed with on the second ascent by C. Read, W. Young on 13.10.73.	
1969	Oct. 12. Manhanger	M. Goff K. Bowden
1970	June. Geodesic	I. Roper C. H. Taylor
1970	Aug. 29. Existentialism	M. A. Toole
1971	May 22. Pisgah Ya Bas	R. Valentine J. Wilkinson B. R. Fuller
1971	July 18. Amoeba	R. Matheson C. A. G. Morton G. Fleming
1971	Aug. 23. Central Buttress Girdle	C. J. S. Bonnington M. Thompson
	20.5.72 Variation I. Roper, C. H. Taylor.	
1971	Sept. 11. The White Wizard	C. J. S. Bonnington N. Estcourt Varied Leads
	25.8.73 Direct Finish C. Read and W. Robinson. Alternate leads.	

1971	Sept. 12. The Gripe	R. Valentine J. Wilkinson D. Pogson
1971	Sept. Last Stand	H. I. Banner M. P. Hatton
	7.10.72 Initial slab climbed by J. Lamb, W. Young, A. Hunter.	
1972	March 25. Moss	M. R. Myers T. W. Birkett
1972	Aug. 26. Incubus	C. Read J. Adams Alternate Leads
1972	Aug. 28. Banner's Exit to Moss Ghyll	H. I. Banner A. N. Other
1972	Aug. 29. Leftovers	R. Bennett Miss R. Lavender
1972	Sept. 30. Westpoint	W. Young M. J. Burbage J. Workman Alternate Leads
1973	May 5. Clockwork Orange	M. J. Burbage W. Young Alternate Leads
1973	June 16. Edge Hog	T. W. Birkett M. R. Myers C. J. Richardson Alternate Leads
1973	Aug. 12. Grand Slam	W. Young I. Singleton Varied Leads
	A point of aid used on pitch 4 was dispensed with on the second ascent. J. Lamb and J. Adams 23.3.1974.	
1974	May 5. The Cumbrian Esk Buttress	R. Valentine P. Braithwaite Alternate leads

MOUNTAIN ACCIDENTS

In dealing with an injured person the aim throughout should be to make him as comfortable as possible and convey him safely and expeditiously off the mountain. Circumstances are different in every case, but the following information should be a guide to those who are called upon to help. This is given in more detail in the booklet 'Mountain Rescue' issued by the Mountain Rescue Committee.

First Steps

First make the injured person as warm and comfortable as possible. His body should be insulated from the cold by heather, bracken or clothing. First aid should be given, the principles of which are described below.

Where a fracture is suspected there is danger in moving the patient and this should be kept to an absolute minimum until the arrival of the stretcher. However, exposure is a serious hazard and if this is likely to be long it may be necessary to get him to a more sheltered situation, to await the rescue party.

If he has to be left alone, while help is organised, it is vital that he should be tied safely to the rock so that he cannot fall further; this is of supreme importance if he is unconscious.

The position must be noted accurately, using compass bearings if necessary, and marked conspicuously if possible.

With an inexperienced group the leader should see the remainder to safe ground.

Organisation of Help

If there is doubt about sending for help do not wait too long in making a decision. Although calling out a rescue party should not be undertaken lightly, the best rule is to send in good time if there is any possibility that help will be needed. The procedure for calling for help is outlined in the following section and should be carefully followed. The messenger should carry full details of time, nature and place of accident. The Mountain Rescue Teams are the main source of help. Their knowledge and skilful handling may be vital to the patient and worth a little delay.

Transport of the Injured

The main principles are:—

Give first aid and immobilise fractured limb.

See that patient is comfortable and warm and securely fixed to the stretcher, making use of the double thigh splint.

No weight should fall on an injured limb during transport.

Reliefs are needed for stretcher carriers.

Provided patient is comfortable, stretcher can be dragged as sledge on easy ground.

N.B.—In spinal and head injuries, stretcher should be kept as level as possible and special care taken to avoid jolts.

FIRST AID

The following is an outline of principles to be observed in the absence of a doctor.

Before touching the patient, enquire and look to decide if spine may be injured. Pain in the back is suggestive.

Pain, Shock and Exposure

Make patient as warm as possible by all available means. If conscious, give hot drinks and glucose frequently unless internal injury is suspected.

Morphia

DO NOT give morphia:—

1. If there are severe head injuries.
2. Where the patient is unconscious.

Morphia is available to relieve pain. Give one ampoule and repeat in one hour if necessary. For children under twelve give only one injection of one half ampoule. Insert needle under pinched-up skin on outer side of arm.

Wounds

Apply "Shell' dressing or gauze and wool then bandage. Do not plug non-bleeding wounds.

Bleeding

If there is severe bleeding do not give stimulants; it is better to give morphia. Plug the wound with gauze, or put on a shell dressing, and if that does not stop the bleeding, put on another. The application of a tourniquet in the form of a scarf or bandage with underlying padding can be very dangerous and should be used only as a last resort when bleeding is very severe and all other attempts to control it have failed. It should be released slowly after fifteen minutes and re-applied if necessary. Pressure at the bleeding point is the best way to stop bleeding.

Fractures

Splint the limb if you can, improvising splints if necessary, the object being to prevent movement of the broken bone and so avoid pain and therefore shock.

Arm.—An angular splint is used on inside of the arm and a short straight splint on outside, clothes or padding intervening. Bandage firmly from shoulder to wrist. It is usually best to fix arm tightly to the chest.

Collar-bone.—Place hand near opposite collar-bone and bind whole shoulder and limb to the chest.

Leg.—Insert boot through circle of Thomas iron by splint (short iron on inside) and pass loop up leg until patient is sitting on ring. Fasten firmly to boot by attached gaiter or rope. Then pass a rope through gaiter strap or loops and, pulling carefully on boot of injured leg, fasten this rope to bottom end of splint, under tension. Pass a continuous bandage or improvise with scarves, puttees or rope, round the leg and splint from groin to boot, so that splint and limb are in one solid piece.

Ankle.—Unlace boot but leave it on leg. Immobilise the limb as above.

Spine.—This injury demands the greatest care of all. Any movement is dangerous. If patient is unconscious look for signs to suggest back injury. If there is the least suspicion that the spine is fractured assume that it is.

The cardinal rule is to try to prevent the slightest bending of the spine in any direction. The casualty must not be moved at all without a proper stretcher and plenty of help and he must be handled throughout with the utmost gentleness. The position of his back must be retained on the stretcher, using all available cushioning.

Unconscious patients

Do not give morphia.

Remove dentures.

If patient is breathing with difficulty this may be relieved by pulling tongue forward, also by turning him on his side.

FIRST AID POSTS and MOUNTAIN RESCUE

In the Lake District, as in all other mountainous parts of Great Britain, first aid equipment has been placed at many strategic points for the use of those concerned in the rescue of the injured. These First Aid Posts have been established through the Mountain Rescue Committee of the Climbing Clubs, with the help of many other people.

Except where otherwise stated, the equipment consists of a stretcher and two rucksacks containing the medical supplies. **Both rucksacks must be taken to a rescue and before leaving base, stimulants, food, sugar and hot drinks must be added.**

In case of emergency on the fells, do not waste time looking for a Mountain Rescue Team, ambulance or doctor. Instead, go to the nearest telephone and ring the *POLICE*, giving as much information of the incident as possible. The police, with their up-to-date knowledge of the availability of the rescue services will quickly organise the appropriate help.

Mountain Rescue Teams, covering the Scafell Group, are based on

Keswick
Eskdale Outward Bound Mountain School
Langdale

In addition, stretchers and other first aid kit are at present available at the following places. These however are not always manned and changes occur from time to time. It should therefore be stressed that in serious cases a team should be contacted through the police.

Mickledore
Styhead Pass
Eskdale Outward Bound Mountain School
Wastwater Hotel
Seathwaite Farm, Borrowdale

Many other teams are available for large rescues and searches. Lists of these are held by the police (through whom calls should be made), and by the Secretary of the Search Panel of the Lake District Mountain Accidents Association (Mr. R. Cook, Watendlath, Ferney Green, Windermere. Telephone: Windermere 3486).

REPORT OF ACCIDENTS

Brief details of all accidents should be reported to the Hon. Secretary of the Mountain Rescue Committee, 9 Milldale Avenue, Temple Meads, Buxton, Derbyshire. Telephone: Buxton 3161.

Equipment should be carefully checked after use and deficiencies or damage of equipment should be reported to the supervisor or the Hon. Secretary of the Mountain Rescue Committee.

Where morphia has been used it is imperative that details be sent immediately to the Hon. Secretary of the Committee at the above address. Every ampoule must be accounted for.

ESK BUTTRESS

The Cumbrian 455 feet. Extremely severe.
High on the face of The Central Pillar is a prominent leftward-slanting cleft. The climb starts up The Central Pillar, then trends left to enter the cleft, the last outstanding problem on the crag, which gives a superb climb at great exposure: considerably harder than The Central Pillar.

1 90 feet.
2 80 feet.
3 70 feet.
4 45 feet.
5 70 feet.
} As for the corresponding pitches of The Central Pillar.

6 70 feet. From the stance on the arête, traverse left; then climb the steep wall to approach the foot of the groove (two nuts for aid), reach across to place a piton in the groove, and with its aid, establish a position in the groove. Continue up the groove, with difficulty, to the bulge, which is surmounted and a small stance is reached, (piton and nut belays).

7 30 feet. Move up; then cross the left wall to gain the arête.
R. Valentine and P. Braithwaite (alternate leads) May 5th, 1974.

Index

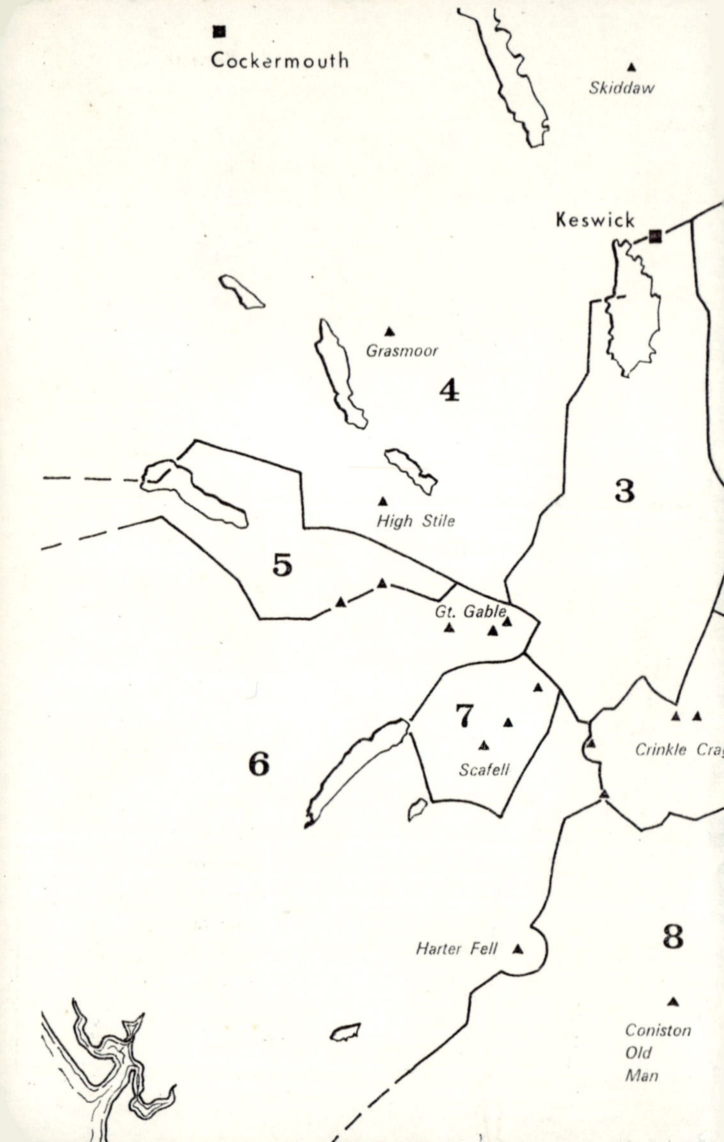
Cockermouth
Skiddaw
Keswick
Grasmoor
4
High Stile
3
5
Gt. Gable
7
6
Scafell
Crinkle Cra
Harter Fell
8
Coniston
Old
Man